GREETINGS FROM

THIS MODERN WORLD

GREETINGS FROM

THIS MODERN WORLD

CARTOONS BY TOM TOMORROW
ST. MARTIN'S PRESS · NEW YORK

 For information, address St. Martin's Press, 175 Fifth Avenue, New York, N.Y. 10010.

Library of Congress Cataloging-in-Publication Data

Tomorrow, Tom
Greetings from this modern world / Tom Tomorrow ; introd. by Bill Griffith.
p. cm.
ISBN 0-312-08203-7
I. Title.
PN6727.T66G74 1992
741.5'973—dc20 92-19913
CIP

10 9 8 7 6 5 4 3 2

I owe a lot of people thanks, and I'd like to mention at least a few of them, in no particular order: my editors at St. Martin's, Abigail Kamen and Alex Kuczynski; all the newspaper editors who have looked at this strange comic strip over the past few years and decided to give it some of their limited and valuable space; my folks, from whom I inherited, through heredity or environment, the cynicism which made *This Modern World* possible in the first place; Bill Griffith, for endless advice (and endless patience); Chas Bufe and Chris Carlsson, for production help and much support; Raymond Larrett, Mike Griffin, and Paola Coda, who have all helped in one way or another; and of course Kimberly, who at one point believed more strongly in the strip than I did. This book is dedicated to her.

To correspond with Tom Tomorrow or get information about running *This Modern World* in *your* newspaper, write Box 170515, S.F., CA 94117.

This Modern World postcards are available from Preziosi Postcards, Box 498, Mendham, N.J. 07945. (Send two stamps for a catalog.) A Tom Tomorrow t-shirt is available from Fairness and Accuracy in Reporting (F.A.I.R.), 130 W. 25th St., New York, NY 10001. A single copy of *Processed World* can be ordered by sending five bucks to their office at 1095 Market St. #210, S.F., CA 94103. Anyone who hates their job should do this posthaste.

INTRODUCTION

by Bill Griffith

I like Tom Tomorrow. He thinks like me. He even hides behind an alter-ego like me. (Come out from behind your punk sunglasses and penguin costume, Dan Perkins!) He borrows tacky media icons from the past to subvert tacky media icons from the present. He lures us into a familiar, fifties clip-art world and, once we're at home in its "safe" surroundings, he delivers his one-two punch to the cultural midsection. He doesn't exactly hold up a mirror to reality—it's more like the glare off a television screen. Am I uttering sound bites yet?

Like most ironic, cool, detached, self-centered, cynical members of the first TV generation, Dan Perkins is a closet optimist. Good satire works like a neutron bomb: it levels institutions, but lets people live. In order to avoid mere ranting or carping, a satirist needs a measure of affection for his target. I was once asked after a talk, "Do you think people are essentially good or essentially evil?" (I should stress that not all my post-lecture questions are this lofty.) I quipped back, "I guess I think people are essentially good enough to make fun of."

Beneath the vicious, unflinching attack on every treasured illusion we Americans hold dear, I believe Dan Perkins also thinks we're good enough to make fun of. Not that he lets such friendly feelings get in the way of the full, frontal assault. His is really the only rational response to This Modern World, after all. We swim in a sea of media. Sam Donaldson is more real to us than our own families. "Infomercials" are the perfect metaphor for our data-based environment: they blur distinctions between entertainment and "news," between fiction and reality. The sea of media forms and informs us. Without unprogrammed "station breaks" like *This Modern World* and other "outsider" views, we'd be sucked into a whirlpool of Bush-speak, neon skiwear, and Dan Rather blather. What *is* the frequency, Kenneth?

As Zippy once put it, "America. I love it, I hate it, I love it, I hate it. When do I collect unemployment?"

Another thing I like about Tom Tomorrow—he wields a mean Toshiba copier.

FOREWORD

by Tom Tomorrow

Yes, Tom Tomorrow is a pseudonym.

It's not because I'm in the witness protection program, nor to protect my secret identity as a costumed crime fighter. It goes back to *This Modern World*'s earliest incarnation, a satire on technology and consumerism gone awry set in a visual clip-art world of fifties futurism, which first appeared in a San Francisco-based magazine called *Processed World. PW* is a sort of journal for radical and disenfranchised office workers and other proletariat of the information age. It often features brutally honest critiques of the angst, despair, and drudgery of the office routine, and examines the small ways in which people trapped in those routines fight back and try to maintain their sanity. There was, at that point, a sense that perhaps it would be best if your boss was not aware of the things you were writing for this magazine, lest you lose your job or get blacklisted by your temp agency as a result of your "bad attitude"—so pen names abounded. Mine stuck.

This Modern World's transition from its focus on consumer society to its current incarnation as a strip of media criticism and political satire was a gradual one, and is documented somewhat by this book. However, there was one event which, in retrospect, marked the transformation into my current, somewhat uneasy identity as a "political cartoonist."

It was the first Saturday after the start of that six-week spasm of mindless patriotic fervor known as the Gulf War, and after spending the day doing my bit for participatory democracy, expressing my opinion in the streets of San Francisco with 100,000 or so of my fellow citizens, I went home and turned on the TV—because, of course, nothing is real in This Modern World until it's been viewed through the eyes of a TV anchorperson. The anchorperson I tuned into reported on the protesters for a minute or two, and then *quickly cut away* to a segment of equal or greater length on the antics of a dozen or so *pro-war* protesters in some conservative bedroom community outside the city. And that was the end of the report. I was outraged at this effective trivialization of the opinions of some 100,000 Americans. My first reaction was to phone the station and lambast a recording machine, which turned out to be less than satisfying...and then it occurred to me that I had a public forum. I went into my studio and wrote the strip that appears on page 53 of this book, and, for better or worse, set foot on a slippery slope from which I have yet to recover.

I've made one more change to the strip since then—the addition of a bitter, sarcastic, wise-cracking penguin named Sparky™. I found that I had set a sort of trap for myself within the parameters of the clip-art world I had established. My characters had always been culled from old advertisements (through a collage-and-copy, pen-and-ink process involving no computers, thank you). I appropriated their obscene cheerfulness for my own ends, but for the satire to be effective, they had to stay in character *("Gosh Biff, isn't the President's new policy terrific?").* I wanted to be more blunt sometimes, and so

Sparky™ was born, unafraid to point out that, for instance, the President is a wanker. (I was recently gratified to learn that Sparky™'s angry attitude is actually scientifically on target; *The New York Times* reports that "popular opinion notwithstanding, these are not friendly birds. They're strong, tough, and aggressive, qualities essential to survival in such a hostile environment." The *Times* was referring to the hostile environment of the Antarctic, but life under three successive Republican administrations hasn't exactly been a cakewalk for Spark—or me either, for that matter.)

Every day, one reads of new outrages, acts of hypocrisy and greed and cynicism committed in the name of goodness, of morality, of the national interest. I think everyone has a different defense mechanism for dealing with these bleak dispatches, defined largely by the circumstances of his or her life—from self-serving rationalizations to utter, impotent rage. There's a street person who spends every day on a bench at the end of Market Street in San Francisco, shouting unintelligibly at the tourists waiting in line at the cable car turnaround. He'll sit quietly for a moment and then suddenly and with no apparent provocation, explode: "Blitherdegrumbledeblather GEORGE BUSH mumbledeblatherdeblither CIA!!" He repeats the same phrase all day long, at maybe thirty-second intervals, and is back the next day with a new and equally cryptic message. I've often thought that if I didn't have the comic strip, that's how I would have eventually ended up—screaming at the world with such bottled-up rage and frustration that the words themselves are made irrelevant. Fortunately for my loved ones, I *do* have the comic strip, and have learned to channel my anger through it—and I hope that to some extent it serves this purpose for my readers as well. I seriously doubt that reading *This Modern World* is going to lead Robert Novak or Pat Buchanan, or any of their ilk, to reexamine their underlying ideological assumptions, but maybe—just maybe—it will help readers with a world-view similar to my own to turn *their* rage at the world into a laugh—rather than an ulcer....

—Dan Perkins
("Tom Tomorrow")
San Francisco, March, 1992

THIS MODERN WORLD by TOM TOMORROW

"THIS MODERN WORLD" IS BUILT UPON A FIRM FOUNDATION OF ***RATIONAL THOUGHT*** AND ***SCIENTIFIC INQUIRY!*** IF NOT FOR DEDICATED SCIENTISTS WORKING TIRELESSLY TO BRING ***ORDER*** AND ***REASON*** TO A CHAOTIC UNIVERSE, WE WOULDN'T HAVE TOASTER OVENS OR COLOR TEEVEES OR ***ANYTHING!***

WE ALL OWE SCIENCE A HECK OF A LOT... BELIEVE ME, I KNOW! YOU SEE, I WAS BORN COLOR BLIND, AND IF IT WEREN'T FOR THIS MODERN-AGE MIRACLE HERE ON MY BACK, I'D BE COMPLETELY UNABLE TO SEE THE COLOR RED!
HEY, MODERN CITIZEN! HAVE YOU THANKED A SCIENTIST... TODAY?

THIS MODERN WORLD by TOM TOMORROW

IN ***THIS MODERN WORLD***, FRIENDS AND RELATIVES ARE NEVER MORE THAN A ***SATELLITE COMMUNICATION LINK*** AWAY! SO GO ON! PICK UP THE TELEPHONE AND CALL SOMEONE YOU LOVE! THEY'LL SOUND SO CLOSE, YOU'LL THINK THEY'RE IN THE **SAME ROOM**! AND MAYBE THEY **ARE**! SO WHAT? CALL THEM **ANYWAY**! **IN**STANTANEOUS SATELLITE TRANSMISSION MAKES AN INTER-HOME PHONE CALL ***ALMOST AS EASY*** AS ***SHOUTING ACROSS THE ROOM***!

HI HONEY! HOW ARE YOU?
JUST FINE, DEAR! WILL YOU PLEASE HAND ME MY GLASSES?

THIS MODERN WORLD by TOM TOMORROW

SAFETY TIPS FOR *MODERN* CITIZENS (#42 IN A SERIES): BE SURE NOT TO CONFUSE YOUR ***ELECTRIC RAZOR*** WITH YOUR ***ELECTRIC STEAK KNIFE!***

OOPS...

THIS MODERN WORLD by TOM TOMORROW

THE COMPUTER SYSTEM IS DOWN AT THE SUPER GIANT AMALGAMATED CORPORATION, AND EVERYONE'S ATTEMPTING TO COPE WITH THE SITUATION...
SO-- WHAT IS THIS THING, ANYWAY?
WELL, THE BOOK SAYS IT'S SOME SORT OF BACKUP WORD PROCESSOR!

THIS MODERN WORLD by TOM TOMORROW

HELLO, CITIZENS! YOU KNOW, YOUR GOVERNMENT WANTS YOU TO BE CONTENT! WE DON'T WANT YOU TO BE BOTHERED BY DISTURBING OR UPSETTING IDEAS! THAT'S WHY WE TRY TO HELP YOU WITH OUR OFFICIAL RECOMMENDED READING LIST!
IT'S EASY TO FOLLOW! WE RECOMMEND THAT YOU READ INSTRUCTIONS, DIRECTIONS, AND OFFICIAL ORDERS! WE RECOMMEND THAT YOU DON'T READ ANYTHING ELSE!
THAT'S RIGHT!
AND YOU KNOW WHAT? PRETTY GIRLS LIKE ME DON'T EVEN LIKE WIMPY GUYS WHO SIT AROUND AND READ ALL DAY! NO, SIREE! WE LIKE MANLY GUYS WHO WATCH TEEVEE!
SO REMEMBER! "READING'S A BORE! WATCH TEEVEE MORE!"
A PUBLIC SERVICE MESSAGE FROM YOUR LOCAL ANTI-LITERACY COUNCIL...

THIS MODERN WORLD

by TOM TOMORROW

YOU KNOW, FOLKS, IF IT WEREN'T FOR MODERN TECHNOLOGY, I WOULDN'T BE STANDING HERE TODAY! YOU SEE, I LOST MY ENTIRE HEAD IN A TERRIBLE BATHROOM ACCIDENT-- AND BOY, IT WAS PRETTY TOUCH-AND-GO THERE FOR AWHILE! BUT HIGHLY SKILLED SURGEONS WERE ABLE TO FIT ME WITH THIS ARTIFICIAL HEAD-- AND TODAY, I LEAD A PERFECTLY NORMAL LIFE! IN FACT, THIS HEAD OF MINE HAS SOME REAL ADVANTAGES! FOR ONE THING, I CAN WATCH MY FAVORITE MORNING BROADCASTS IN THE BATH-ROOM MIRROR WHILE I GET READY FOR WORK EACH DAY! AND-- BEST OF ALL--MY WIFE NEVER TIRES OF GAZING LOVINGLY INTO MY EYES--DO YOU, HONEY?
I CERTAINLY DON'T, DEAR! BECAUSE IF I DO, I JUST CHANGE THE CHANNEL!

THIS MODERN WORLD by TOM TOMORROW

HI, FOLKS! YOU KNOW, UNOCCUPIED MINDS ARE THE DEVIL'S PLAYGROUND! SURE, YOU STAY BUSY AT WORK OR SCHOOL ALL DAY, BUT WHAT DO YOU DO WITH YOUR LEFTOVER TIME? DO YOU FIND YOURSELF EXPERIENCING SUCH OLD-FASHIONED EMOTIONS AS BOREDOM OR DEPRESSION? WELL, THERE'S CERTAINLY NO NEED FOR THAT IN THIS MODERN WORLD!
THAT'S FOR SURE! WE LIKE TO AVOID UNPLEASANT, COUNTER-PRODUCTIVE EXISTENTIAL DESPAIR BY KICKING BACK IN THE EVENING WITH A VARIETY OF OUR FAVORITE SNACK PRODUCTS AND TURNING ON ALL OF OUR TEEVEES AND RADIOS AT ONCE!
YES-- EACH TUNED TO A DIFFERENT STATION! AND WE'RE PROUD OF OUR INFORMATION CONSUMPTION! WHY, DID YOU KNOW THAT SUCH SUPPOSEDLY WISE MEN AS PLATO AND SOCRATES WOULD HAVE BEEN COMPLETELY UNABLE TO COPE WITH MORE THAN TWO SIMULTANEOUS BROADCASTS? HA, HA, HA!
YOU'VE GOT TO BUY--
CHUCKLE!
--AND BUY--
--AND BUY!

THIS MODERN WORLD by TOM TOMORROW

WORRIED ABOUT YOUR SMOKING HABITS? WELL, DON'T BE *SILLY!* LIGHT UP ANOTHER CIGARETTE AND *RELAX!* WE NO LONGER LIVE IN THE *DARK AGES*, HUDDLED AROUND A METAPHORICAL *CAMPFIRE* IN FEAR OF *LUNG CANCER* OR *EMPHYSEMA!* WE'VE GOT *MODERN MEDICAL TECHNOLOGY* ON OUR SIDE! OUR SOPHISTICATED EQUIPMENT CAN SUSTAIN EVEN THE MOST *RAVAGED*, *DISEASED* CARCASS--*INDEFINITELY!* SO-- NOT TO WORRY! *ENJOY LIFE!* SMOKE MORE *CIGARETTES!*

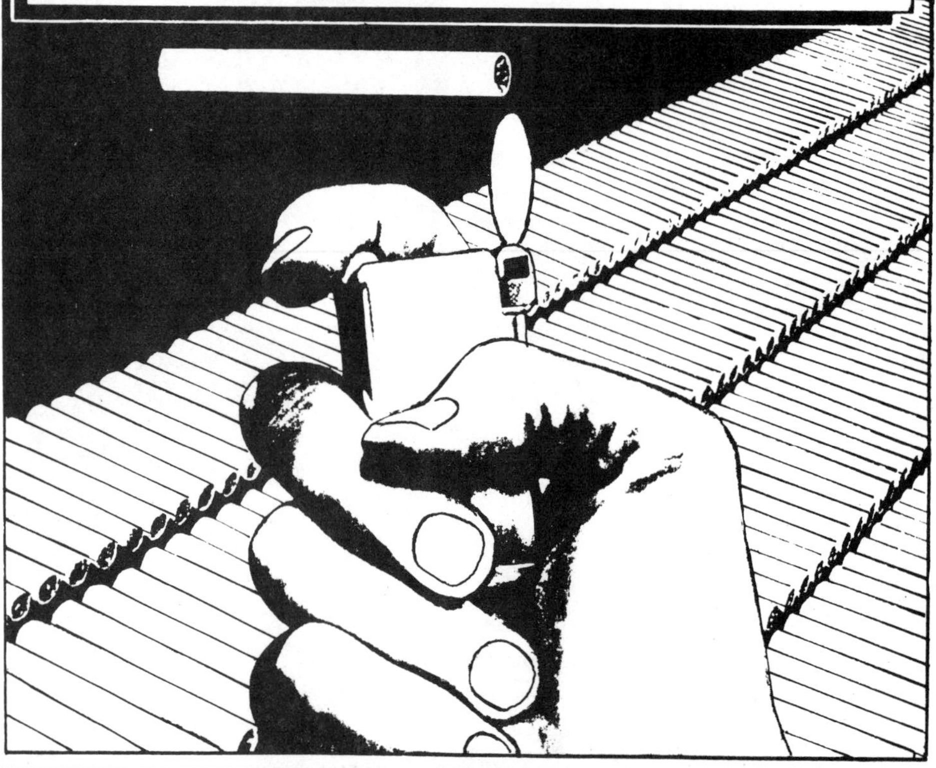

JUST LISTEN TO WHAT THESE FAMOUS PEOPLE SAY!
SMOKE!
SMOKE!
SMOKE!
SMOKE!

THIS MODERN WORLD by TOM TOMORROW

IT'S THE *LATEST RAGE* FROM PARIS-ELEGANT EVENING WEAR DESIGNED AFTER YOUR *FAVORITE SNACK PRODUCT!*

THE DESIGN YOU CHOOSE MAKES A *UNIQUELY PERSONAL* FASHION STATEMENT!

AFTER ALL-AS CONSUMERS IN GAY PAREE ARE SAYING THIS SEASON--"YOU ARE WHAT YOU EAT, *N'EST-CE PAS?*"

Sunshine
Hi Ho
CRACKERS
Hires
ROOT BEER
WITH REAL ROOT JUICES

THIS MODERN WORLD by TOM TOMORROW

UH OH! LOOKS LIKE BILL'S BEEN FORGETTING TO TAKE HIS MEMORY ENHANCEMENT PILLS!
DRAT! WHAT WAS I GOING TO SAY?!
IT WAS RIGHT ON THE TIP OF MY...
MY...
YOU KNOW, THAT THING IN MY MOUTH...

THIS MODERN WORLD by TOM TOMORROW
WHY, IT'S BILL 43480, CHEERFULLY SUBMITTING TO AN INGESTED SUBSTANCES TEST!
THAT'S RIGHT! I'M MORE THAN HAPPY TO PUT UP WITH SUCH A MINOR INCONVENIENCE IF IT HELPS KEEP MY COUNTRY-- AND MY CORPORATION-- STRONG! AFTER ALL, THE INNOCENT HAVE NOTHING TO HIDE--RIGHT?
PRELIMINARY ANALYSIS
SUBJECT: BILL 43480
ALCOHOL: 89%
CAFFEINE: 93%
TOBACCO: 94%
MISC. CARCINOGENS: 86%
THAT'S RIGHT, BILL! AND IT LOOKS LIKE YOU'RE AS INNOCENT AS THEY COME! JUST LOOK AT THAT READOUT! YOUR LEVELS ARE WELL ABOVE MINIMUM STANDARDS FOR INGESTION OF ALCOHOL, CAFFEINE, TOBACCO, AND ALL OTHER REQUIRED SUBSTANCES!

THIS MODERN WORLD by TOM TOMORROW

HONEY— WILL YOU JOIN ME IN REGISTERING OUR LOVE WITH THE APPROPRIATE GOVERN-MENTAL BUREAUCRACIES?
OH JIM, YOU ROMANTIC FOOL -- OF COURSE I'LL MARRY YOU!
©1990 TOM TOMORROW

THIS MODERN WORLD by TOM TOMORROW

YOUR GAS TANK IS LIKE A *BARREN LAKE BED!*
SERVICE WITH A SIMILE.

THIS MODERN WORLD by TOM TOMORROW

IT'S COFFEE THAT FUELS THE WHEELS OF INDUSTRY IN THIS MODERN WORLD, AND KEEPS THEM TURNING AROUND AND AROUND AND AROUND AND AROUND! YES, THAT'S RIGHT-- COFFEE! LOTS AND LOTS OF COFFEE! AND DON'T YOU FORGET IT! BECAUSE YOU'RE NOT GOING TO GET ANYWHERE WITHOUT DRINKING A WHOLE LOT OF COFFEE!

SO IF YOU'RE FEELING TIRED... RUN DOWN... UNPRODUCTIVE... WELL DRINK SOME MORE COFFEE AND GET BACK TO WORK!

HANDY COFFEE DRINKING TIP: THERE'S NOTHING LIKE A HEAPING SPOONFUL OF NON-DAIRY COFFEE WHITENER TO MAKE YOUR COFFEE AT LEAST LOOK LIKE IT HAS CREAM IN IT.

THIS MODERN WORLD

by TOM TOMORROW

HELLO, CITIZENS! WE'VE HEARD REPORTS THAT SOME *ALARMISTS* ARE UPSET BY OUR RECENT DISPLAYS OF *MILITARY SUPERIORITY!* WELL, *DON'T WORRY!* IT'S ALL PART OF OUR CARE-FULLY CON-CEIVED POLICY OF *CONSTRUC-TIVE DESTRUC-TION!*

YES, THAT'S RIGHT! YOU SEE, THE COUNTRIES WE'VE BEEN ATTACKING ARE OUR *VILE ENEMIES!* THEIR SOCIETIES ARE BASED ON ECONOMIC SYSTEMS *DIFF-ERENT* FROM OURS!

AND AS DESPICABLE AND UNDER-HANDED AS WE KNOW THEM TO BE, WE WERE QUITE SURE *THEY* PLANNED TO ATTACK *US* WITHOUT WARN-ING OR PROV-OCATION! WE THEREFORE FELT IT NEC-ESSARY TO LAUNCH A *PURELY DEFENSIVE* PRE-EMPTIVE *FIRST STRIKE!*

YES, AND WE DID IT FOR *YOU!* SO WHEN THE CURFEW BELLS RING TO-NIGHT, YOU CAN REST WELL-- SECURE IN THE KNOWLEDGE THAT YOUR MILITARY IS EVER-VIGILANTLY GUARDING *YOUR* ECONOMIC SYSTEM!

GOOD NIGHT, AND REMEMBER-CHECK THOSE RADIATION LEVELS BEFORE VEN-TURING *OUTSIDE!*

THIS MODERN WORLD by TOM TOMORROW

HELLO, BIFF! WHAT ARE YOU DOING?

HELLO, BETTY! I'M ABOUT TO EXPRESS MY CONTEMPT FOR OUR CONSUMER-BASED ECONOMY WITH MY PURCHASE OF THIS ***PUNK ROCK ALBUM!***

HEY, THAT'S GREAT! I MYSELF PLAN LATER TO SHOP FOR SOME SCREEN PRINTED T-SHIRTS WHICH BEAR ***REBELLIOUS MESSAGES*** APPROPRIATE TO MY ***NON-CONFORMIST PHILOSOPHY!***

PUNK'S NOT DEAD

THIS MODERN WORLD by TOM TOMORROW

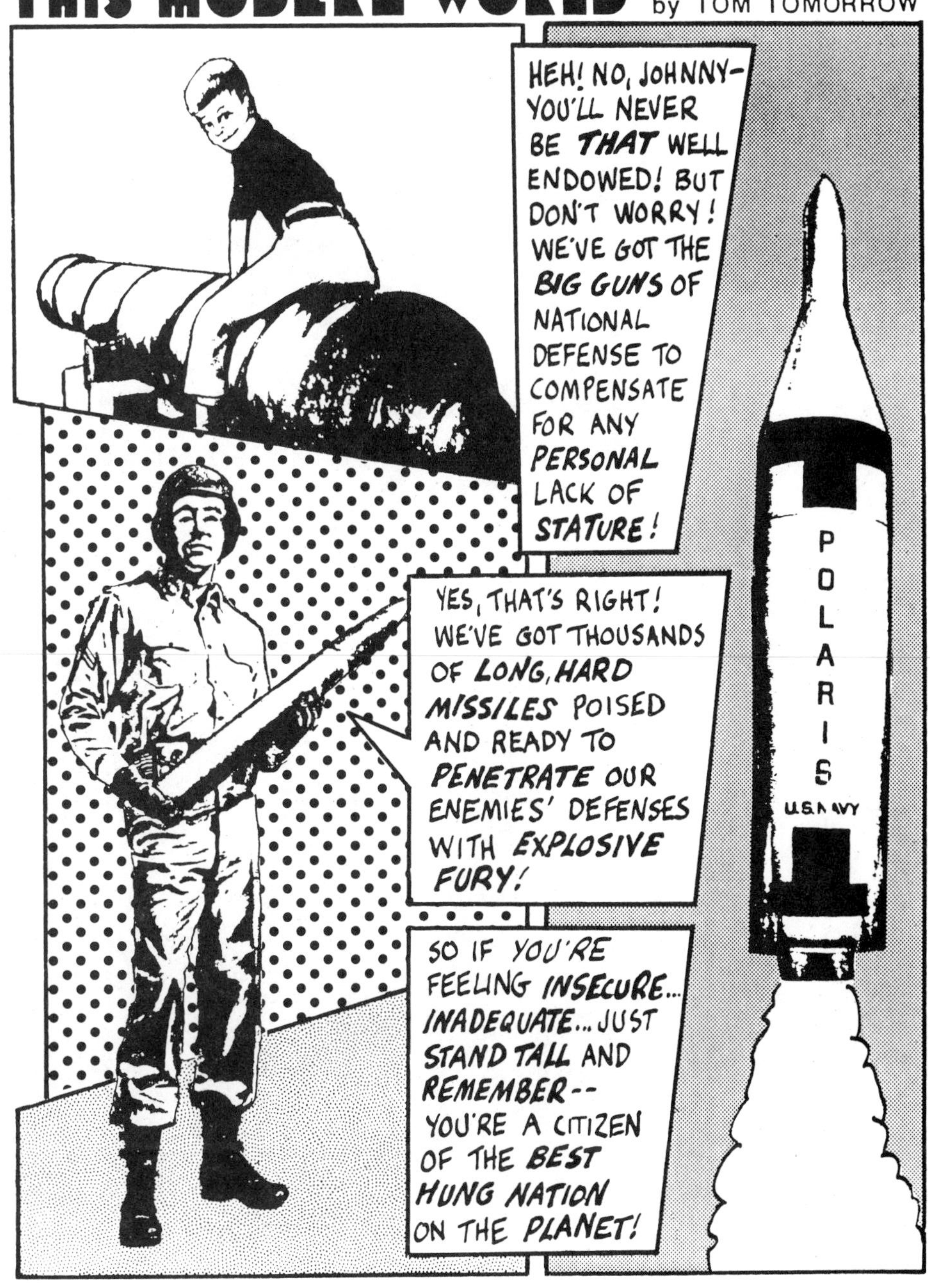

HEH! NO, JOHNNY- YOU'LL NEVER BE THAT WELL ENDOWED! BUT DON'T WORRY! WE'VE GOT THE BIG GUNS OF NATIONAL DEFENSE TO COMPENSATE FOR ANY PERSONAL LACK OF STATURE!
YES, THAT'S RIGHT! WE'VE GOT THOUSANDS OF LONG, HARD MISSILES POISED AND READY TO PENETRATE OUR ENEMIES' DEFENSES WITH EXPLOSIVE FURY!
SO IF YOU'RE FEELING INSECURE... INADEQUATE... JUST STAND TALL AND REMEMBER-- YOU'RE A CITIZEN OF THE BEST HUNG NATION ON THE PLANET!
POLARIS
U.S. NAVY

THIS MODERN WORLD by TOM TOMORROW

OKAY, LISTEN UP, SON. "EAT YOUR VEGETABLES"! THAT'S DADDY'S SOUND BITE FOR THE DAY! "EAT YOUR VEGETABLES"! GOT THAT?
YES, DAD! DO WE HAVE A PHOTO OP TO GO WITH THAT?

THIS MODERN WORLD

by TOM TOMORROW

HELLO, AND WELCOME TO ANOTHER EDITION OF "WHAT TV CELEBRITIES THINK ABOUT IMPORTANT WORLD EVENTS"! THIS WEEK: VANNA WHITE!
ON THE PALESTINIAN UPRISING:
I THINK EVERYONE SHOULD LEARN TO LIVE TOGETHER AND BE FRIENDS AND STUFF.
ON TOXIC WASTE:
I THINK IT'S BAD BECAUSE WE ALL HAVE TO BREATHE THE AIR AND DRINK THE WATER AND STUFF.
ON THE ARMS RACE:
I THINK NUCLEAR WAR IS BAD BECAUSE EVERYONE WOULD DIE AND STUFF.
WELL, THAT'S IT FOR THIS WEEK! SO REMEMBER--TV CELEBRITIES KNOW MORE ABOUT LIFE THAN YOU! AFTER ALL...THEY'RE FAMOUS!

THIS MODERN WORLD by TOM TOMORROW

HELLO EVERYONE! I'D LIKE TO THANK YOU FOR ATTENDING *THIS MODERN WORLD'S "STANDUP COMEDY NIGHT"*! HEY! I'D LIKE TO MAKE A *SLY REFERENCE* TO ALCOHOL'S TENDENCY TO LOOSEN INHIBITIONS! ALL RIGHT!
HA HA HA HA HA

SAY! HOW ABOUT A COMMONLY SHARED EXPERIENCE SUCH AS RIDING ON AIRPLANES *OR* GETTING UP EARLY IN THE MORNING! *HEY!*
HA HA HA HA HA

AREN'T THERE QUITE A LOT OF AMUSING ASPECTS TO THAT EXPERIENCE? YOU BET! *HOO BOY!* AND JUST IMAGINE THOSE AMUSING ASPECTS CARRIED OUT TO *RIDICULOUS EXTREMES*! HA, HA! HEY!
HA HA HA HA HA

WOW! NOW IT'S TIME TO ACKNOWLEDGE AND CONCLUDE THE TEMPORARY, SUPERFICIAL BOND BETWEEN AUDIENCE AND PERFORMER! THANKS VERY MUCH! YOU'VE BEEN GREAT!
HA HA HA HA HA

THIS MODERN WORLD by TOM TOMORROW

HEH! GUESS WHAT THIS CIGARETTE IS BIGGER THAN!
WHO ARE YOU TALKING TO, HONEY?

THIS MODERN WORLD by TOM TOMORROW

GOOD NEWS, HONEY! THE MAN FROM THE E.P.A. SAYS THERE'S NOTHING TO WORRY ABOUT!
OH, WHAT A RELIEF!

THIS MODERN WORLD by TOM TOMORROW

beep beep beep beep beep beep beep beep beep
HEY EVERYONE! ANOTHER HOUR OF OUR LIVES HAS PASSED-- NEVER TO BE EXPERIENCED AGAIN!
GOSH, BOB! YOUR DIGITAL BEEPING WATCH SERVES AS A POIGNANT REMINDER OF OUR OWN MORTALITY-- AND HOW TRULY PRECIOUS EACH HOUR IS!
YES--IT ALWAYS MAKES ME THINK OF THE NEED TO LIVE EACH HOUR TO THE FULLEST-- BECAUSE WE DO NOT KNOW HOW MANY REMAIN!
THE HOURLY BEEPING OF BOB'S DIGITAL WATCH ALWAYS CAUSES THE GANG AT THE OFFICE TO PAUSE FOR A REFLECTIVE MOMENT...
©1990 TOM TOMORROW

THIS MODERN WORLD by TOM TOMORROW

IT'S TIME FOR A ***SNEAK PREVIEW*** OF SOME UPCOMING NEW ***T.V. SHOWS!***

"WHY DON'T YOU BUY ONE OF THESE" ... AN ENTERTAINING WEEKLY COMPENDIUM OF CONSUMER GOODS ***YOU*** COULD PURCHASE!

NOW HERE'S A USEFUL ITEM!

"CORPORATE RAP"... THE WACKY MISADVENTURES OF THREE AGING EXECUTIVES WHO FORM A "***POSSE***" AND START "***RAPPIN'***"!

WE'RE RICH OLD WHITE MEN,
AND WE DON'T CARE --
WHAT HAPPENS TWENTY YEARS
FROM NOW,
'CAUSE WE WON'T BE THERE!
HUNH!

"THE KING AND ME"...THE REALLY HIP, POST-MODERN, IRONIC STORY OF -- GET THIS -- ***ELVIS PRESLEY*** AND ***MARILYN MONROE*** FLYING AROUND IN A ***UFO!*** NOT EVEN DAVID LYNCH COULD BE ***THIS*** "FAR OUT"!

LET'S GO TO A 7-11 IN DULUTH AND BUY SOME TWINKIES!

"SUPERMARKET COP"... HIGH TENSION AND EXCITING DRAMA COLLIDE IN THIS FAST-PACED, ACTION-PACKED TALE OF A ***SUPERMARKET SECURITY GUARD!***

HANDS OFF THOSE RUTA-BAGAS, HAIRBALL!
©1991 TOM TOMORROW

THIS MODERN WORLD by TOM TOMORROW

THIS WEEK--A LOOK AT THE AMAZING PROPHECIES OF NOSTRADAMUS!
SPOOKY SOUND EFFECT
OOOO-EEEE-OOOH.

HE PREDICTED THAT ALF WOULD BE A HIT TV SERIES!
OOO-EEE-OOOH

HE PREDICTED THE MILLI VANILLI LIP-SYNCHING SCANDAL!
OOO-EEEE-OOH

HE EVEN PREDICTED THAT YOU WOULD READ THIS CARTOON!
OOOO-EEEE-OOOH
©1991 TOM TOMORROW

THIS MODERN WORLD by TOM TOMORROW

LADIES AND GENTLEMEN...THE PRESIDENT OF THE UNITED STATES...
GOOD EVENING.
LIES, LIES, LIES.

SELF-SERVING HYPOCRITICAL RHETORIC...

...SIMPLISTIC MIS-REPRESENTATIONS OF FACTS...

...NAKED EMOTIONAL APPEALS AND MORE DAMNED LIES.
THANK YOU. GOOD NIGHT.
©1991 TOM TOMORROW

THIS MODERN WORLD

by TOM TOMORROW

WE HERE AT *"THIS MODERN WORLD"* WOULD LIKE TO TAKE THIS OPPORTUNITY TO THANK OUR MANY FRIENDS WHO HAVE SO OFTEN SHARED THEIR MARVELOUS ANECDOTES WHICH WOULD "MAKE A GOOD CARTOON"! WE DON'T KNOW HOW WE COULD POSSIBLY MEET OUR DEADLINES IF IT WEREN'T FOR THE CONSTANT INSPIRATION THESE HUMOROUS STORIES PROVIDE!

...AND I HAD TO WAIT IN LINE AT THE DMV FOR AN HOUR AND THEN IT TURNS OUT I HAD THE WRONG PAPERS! HEY--I BET YOU COULD GET A GOOD CARTOON OUT OF THAT!

...BUT THE LIGHT BULB HAD BURNED OUT, SO I COULDN'T SEE AND I STUBBED MY TOE! HEY--I BET YOU COULD GET A GOOD CARTOON OUT OF THAT!

...AND SO THIS CRAZY PERSON STARTED FOLLOWING ME DOWN THE STREET AND SAYING ALL THESE REALLY WEIRD THINGS! HEY--I BET YOU COULD GET A GOOD CARTOON OUT OF THAT!

THIS MODERN WORLD by TOM TOMORROW

1991: THE MITCHELLS IN FRONT OF THEIR NEWLY-PURCHASED HOME IN LOVE CANAL... WHICH THE GOVERNMENT ASSURES THEM IS NOW COMPLETELY SAFE AND TOXIN-FREE...
1996: THE MITCHELL CHILDREN, EDNA AND JOE-BOB.
©1991 TOM TOMORROW

THIS MODERN WORLD by TOM TOMORROW

HEY, CITIZENS! HAVE YOU EVER WONDERED WHAT'S GOING ON IN YOUR CAT'S TINY LITTLE BRAIN AS IT SITS MOTIONLESS, STARING INTO SPACE? WELL, YOU NEED WONDER NO LONGER, THANKS TO THE HARDWORKING SCIENTISTS IN THE ***T.M.W. LABORATORY COMPLEX*** AND THEIR AMAZING NEW SCIENTIFIC BREAKTHROUGH, THE "***FELINE THOUGHT DECODER***"!

11:00 A.M.
...AND THAT'S THE VARIABLE THE BIG BANG THEORY DOESN'T TAKE INTO ACCOUNT!
WELL, I GUESS I'LL TAKE A NAP NOW.

3:40 P.M.
..AND THEREFORE, THERE IS INHERENTLY NO CONFLICT BETWEEN CARTESIAN AND NEWTONIAN THOUGHT!
I WONDER IF THERE'S ANYTHING TO EAT.

6:20 P.M.
...AND THAT'S THE ONLY COURSE OF ACTION POSSIBLE TO STABILIZE THE CURRENTLY VOLATILE GEOPOLITICAL SCENE!
I THINK I'LL TAKE ANOTHER NAP NOW.

WELL, ITS PRETTY MUCH WHAT YOU PROBABLY FIGURED... CATS SPEND MOST OF THEIR TIME THINKING ABOUT ***EATING*** AND ***SLEEPING***...

THIS MODERN WORLD by TOM TOMORROW

THE WHITE HOUSE "LINE OF THE DAY"-- A SIMPLISTIC MISREPRESENTATION OF FACTS, DESIGNED TO SWAY PUBLIC OPINION...
WE'VE DISCOVERED THAT THE DEMOCRATIC MEMBERS OF CONGRESS ALL WORSHIP SATAN!

IN PRESS CONFERENCES, THE "LINE OF THE DAY" IS REINFORCED THROUGH CONSTANT REPETITION... WORKED INTO EVERY ANSWER, NO MATTER WHAT THE QUESTION MAY BE...

SIR--DO YOU HAVE ANY COMMENT ON THE INCREASING COST OF THE SAVINGS AND LOAN BAILOUT?
WELL--WE'RE WORKING ON THAT--BUT WE NEED THE HELP OF THE CONGRESS--AND I'LL TELL YOU, IT'S NOT EASY TO WORK WITH A BUNCH OF SATANISTS!
WHAT ABOUT THE WORSENING MIDEAST SITUATION?
YOU KNOW--IT'S MIGHTY HOT IN THE DESERT--BUT IT'S HOTTER DOWN IN HELL, HOME OF THE DEMOCRATS' CLOSE PERSONAL FRIEND...SATAN!
FINALLY, IN CASE ANYONE MISSED IT, THE PRESIDENT REITERATES HIS "LINE OF THE DAY" IN HIS CLOSING REMARKS...
NO MORE QUESTIONS--I'VE GOT TO GO! BUT LISTEN--BE CAREFUL AROUND THOSE CONGRESSIONAL DEMOCRATS--UNLESS YOU WANT TO END UP AS A HUMAN SACRIFICE...TO SATAN!
ACHTUNG, CITIZENS! JOSEPH GOEBBELS HERE! REMEMBER-A LIE REPEATED LOUD ENOUGH AND LONG ENOUGH... BECOMES TRUE!
©1990 TOM TOMORROW

THIS MODERN WORLD by TOM TOMORROW

IN ANCIENT TIMES, OUR PRIMITIVE ANCESTORS HUDDLED AROUND THE CAMPFIRE IN FEARFUL IGNORANCE OF THE WORLD AROUND THEM! IN THIS MODERN WORLD, HOWEVER, THE LIGHT OF REASON SHINES BRIGHTLY AS FAMILIES GATHER AROUND THE WARM GLOW OF THEIR TELEVISION SETS!
COMING UP NEXT ON THE NEWS: TERRIFYING, INEXPLICABLE EVENTS OCCURING IN FAR-AWAY PLACES, PRESENTED WITHOUT HISTORICAL OR SOCIOLOGICAL CONTEXT!
GEEZ! IT LOOKS PRETTY BAD OUT THERE!
I'M CERTAINLY GLAD WE'RE SAFE HERE AT HOME!
©1990 TOM TOMORROW

THIS MODERN WORLD

by TOM TOMORROW

HEY, CITIZENS! BY NOW, YOU'VE ALMOST CERTAINLY INTEGRATED MERYL STREEP'S ADVICE ON ENVIRONMENTAL MATTERS INTO YOUR PERSONAL LIVES...

HEY HONEY! WHAT ARE YOU DOING?
WHY, I'M WASHING THESE APPLES TO REMOVE CONTAMINANTS -- LIKE MERYL STREEP SAYS I SHOULD!

...BUT DON'T YOU SOMETIMES WISH YOU KNEW WHAT MERYL STREEP HAD TO SAY ABOUT ***OTHER*** AREAS OF UNCERTAINTY IN LIFE?

GOSH...I WONDER IF MERYL STREEP RECOMMENDS THIS BRAND OF TOOTHPASTE!

WELL ***WONDER NO LONGER*** -- FOR NOW YOU CAN CONSULT THE BRAND NEW ***MERYL STREEP GUIDE TO LIFE!*** IT'S A DICTIONARY-SIZED REFERENCE BOOK FEATURING MERYL STREEP'S ADVICE ON ***EVERY SUBJECT IMAGINABLE*** FROM ***DENTAL CARE*** TO ***CHILD REARING*** TO ***NUCLEAR PHYSICS*** -- JUST TO NAME A ***FEW!***

MERYL STREEP'S GUIDE TO LIFE
MERYL STREEP'S GUIDE TO LIFE

I WONDER IF I SHOULD USE DRYWALL NAILS OR ANCHOR SCREWS TO SECURE THESE SHELVES TO THE WALL!
WELL, HONEY, LET'S...
...SEE WHAT MERYL SAYS!!
THE MERYL STREEP GUIDE TO LIFE -- MERYL SAYS, "BUY IT!"
© 1990 TOM TOMORROW

THIS MODERN WORLD by TOM TOMORROW

GOOD EVENING--I'M TED KOPPEL--
AND I'M TED KOPPEL'S **HAIR!**
HUH?

FOR YEARS, MANY OF YOU HAVE NOTICED SOMETHING VAGUELY AMISS ABOUT TED'S COIFFURE. THERE HAS BEEN MUCH SPECULATION. IS IT A WIG? DOES TED HAVE NO MIRRORS IN HIS HOME?
WELL, THE **TRUTH** OF THE MATTER IS THAT I--TED KOPPEL'S HAIR--AM AN **ALIEN BEING** FROM A **DISTANT PLANET!**

THE PEOPLE OF MY RACE MUST LIVE IN A SYMBIOTIC RELATIONSHIP WITH A HOST BEING IN ORDER TO SURVIVE! I HAVE BEEN AN ADVANCE SCOUT STUDYING YOUR RACE, AND AFTER MANY YEARS, I HAVE DETERMINED THAT WE ARE **QUITE COMPATIBLE!**

EVEN AS I SPEAK, MILLIONS OF MY PEOPLE ARE ON THEIR WAY TO THIS PLANET.
NOW, THE SYMBIOSIS IS HARMLESS TO THE HOST--AND WILL EVEN BE BENEFICIAL, AS WE WILL OF COURSE SHARE OUR ADVANCED KNOWLEDGE OF PHILOSOPHY, SCIENCE AND ART--FOREVER ENDING FAMINE, WAR AND DISEASE ON YOUR PLANET.

THE ONLY DRAWBACK--*heh heh*--IS THAT EVERY HUMAN ON EARTH WILL HAVE HAIR LIKE **TED KOPPEL!**

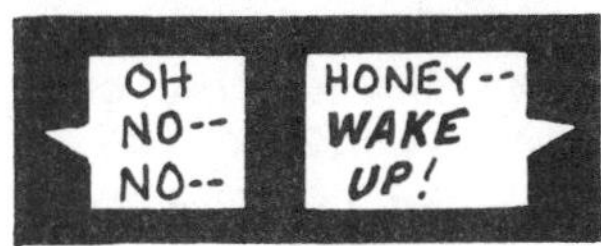
OH NO--NO--
HONEY--**WAKE UP!**

GEEZ--I JUST HAD THE MOST **TERRIBLE NIGHTMARE**--
BILL--WHAT'S THAT THING ON YOUR **HEAD?**
©1991 TOM TOMORROW

THIS MODERN WORLD by TOM TOMORROW

EEEEEEEEEEEE EEEEEEEEEEEEEE
HONEY--LISTEN! DO YOU HEAR THAT NOISE?!
YES! QUICKLY--GO PHONE THE POLICE, WHILE I ATTEMPT TO APPREHEND THE PERPETRATOR!
A TYPICAL SCENE THAT IS REPLAYED EVERY DAY, ALL OVER THIS MODERN WORLD, EACH TIME DILIGENT, LAW-ABIDING CITIZENS ARE ALERTED TO THE POSSIBILITY OF WRONGDOING—BY THE SOUND OF A CAR ALARM!

THIS MODERN WORLD by TOM TOMORROW

HEY CITIZENS! IT'S TIME FOR A SNEAK PREVIEW OF "THOSE TYPING EMERSONS," ABC'S HEARTWARMING NEW SERIES ABOUT A FAMILY THAT LOVES TO TYPE!
HEY EVERYONE-- I'M BORED! LET'S HAVE A TYPING CONTEST!
THAT'S A GREAT IDEA, SIS!
REMEMBER, KIDS-- SPEED COUNTS, BUT SO DOES ACCURACY!
OKAY EVERYBODY-- READY... SET... GO!
WHO WINS? WELL, YOU'LL JUST HAVE TO TUNE IN NEXT SEASON TO FIND OUT! BUT WE WILL SAY THIS-- WITH DAD'S EMPHASIS ON GOOD TYPING SKILLS, EVERYONE'S A WINNER IN THE TYPING EMERSON FAMILY!
©1990 TOM TOMORROW

THIS MODERN WORLD by TOM TOMORROW

GOOD EVENING-I'M DAN RATHER. LEADING OFF THE NEWS TONIGHT, A MAJOR CONFLAGRATION THAT COULD HAVE DECIMATED NEW YORK CITY WAS NARROWLY AVOIDED THIS AFTERNOON!

"...IT WAS 4:00 P.M. IN THE CBS STUDIOS WHEN A TECHNICIAN LIGHTING A CIGARETTE ACCIDENTALLY DROPPED HIS MATCH!"

"HAD THERE BEEN A LARGE STACK OF OLD NEWSPAPERS NEARBY, OR AN OLD PILE OF GASOLINE-SOAKED RAGS, THERE MIGHT HAVE BEEN A FIRE WHICH COULD HAVE DESTROYED THE STUDIOS--AND, IN A WORST-CASE SCENARIO, POSSIBLY MUCH OF NEW YORK CITY!"
(ARTIST'S RENDITION)

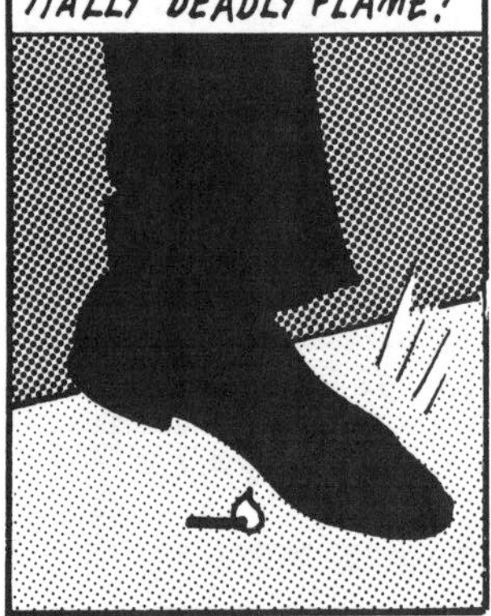
"FORTUNATELY, THERE WAS NO SUCH COMBUSTIBLE MATERIAL NEARBY. THE TECHNICIAN, THINKING QUICKLY, STEPPED ON THE MATCH AND DOUSED THE POTENTIALLY DEADLY FLAME!"

"ONE EXPERT HAD THIS COMMENT..."
I THINK THIS INCIDENT DEMONSTRATES THE NEED FOR STRICTER RULES AND REGULATIONS!
(AN EXPERT)

COMING UP NEXT--THE PRESIDENT STUMBLED ON THE WHITE HOUSE LAWN TODAY. HAD HE FALLEN AND HIT HIS HEAD ON A ROCK, EXPERTS SAY HE MIGHT HAVE DIED.
FIRST, THESE MESSAGES.

THIS MODERN WORLD by TOM TOMORROW

HELLO, CITIZENS! IT'S TIME ONCE AGAIN FOR "ADVICE FOR ORDINARY PEOPLE--FROM CELEBRITIES"--THE PROGRAM THAT HELPS THE STARS HELP YOU HELP YOURSELF! LET'S GET STARTED...
FAMOUS ACTRESS AND SONGSTRESS CHER SAYS:
UM... I THINK YOU SHOULD EAT A BALANCED DIET AND, LIKE, GET PLENTY OF REST...
HEY! THAT'S A GOOD IDEA!
WELL-KNOWN TEEN HEART-THROB MICHAEL J. FOX ADVISES:
BRUSH YOUR TEETH AFTER EVERY MEAL-AND FOR GOSH SAKES DON'T FORGET TO FLOSS!
BOY--THAT'S DARNED GOOD THINKING!
MULTITALENTED SINGING SENSATION GEORGE MICHAEL TELLS US:
UH, I THINK PEOPLE SHOULD EXERCISE, LIKE, EVERY DAY!
YOU KNOW--HE'S RIGHT!
AND LASTLY, LOVABLE "COSBY KID" MALCOM JAMAL WARNER SUGGESTS:
WELL, UM, I THINK PEOPLE SHOULD LOOK BOTH WAYS BEFORE, UM, THEY CROSS THE STREET!
THAT'S PRETTY SENSIBLE!
THAT'S ALL FOR NOW! WE HOPE YOU'VE LEARNED AS MUCH AS WE HAVE!
©1990 TOM TOMORROW

THIS MODERN WORLD by TOM TOMORROW

HEY CITIZENS! IT'S TIME FOR A LOOK AT *U.S. MILITARY INTERVENTION*, AS DEBATED BY THE *EXPERTS* ON *PUBLIC TELEVISION NEWS PROGRAMS!*

WRONG:
I THINK THAT INTERVENTION MAY ONLY SERVE TO ESCALATE HOSTILITIES!
I'M AFRAID I HAVE TO DISAGREE! INTERVENTION IS NECESSARY TO CONTROL FURTHER AGGRESSION!

RIGHT:
I THINK WE SHOULD DROP A NUCLEAR BOMB!
I'M AFRAID I HAVE TO DISAGREE! I THINK WE SHOULD DROP SEVERAL NUCLEAR BOMBS!
©1990 TOM TOMORROW

THIS MODERN WORLD by TOM TOMORROW

WHAT IF ***THIS COMIC STRIP*** WERE RUN LIKE THE ***MOVIE BUSINESS?***

FIRST, THE INITIAL CARTOON WOULD BE SUBMITTED...

THIS MODERN WORLD
HEY CITIZENS! WHY DID THE CHICKEN CROSS THE ROAD?
TO GET TO THE OTHER SIDE!

THEN, THE PROCESS OF ***REVISIONS*** WOULD BEGIN...

I ***LOVE*** IT, BABE! IT JUST NEEDS A LITTLE MORE... ***SEX APPEAL!*** MAYBE WE COULD GIVE THE CHICKEN A ***GIRLFRIEND*** WHO ALWAYS WEARS A ***BIKINI!***

IT'S A ***FANTASTIC*** CARTOON! IT'S JUST THAT... WELL... WE DID SOME FOCUS GROUPS, AND THE CHICKEN JUST DIDN'T GO OVER TOO WELL... BUT ***PENGUINS*** WERE ***REALLY POPULAR!*** DO YOU THINK WE COULD MAKE THE CHICKEN A ***PENGUIN?***

THIS IS UNDOUBTEDLY ONE OF THE ***BEST*** CARTOONS I'VE EVER SEEN... I REALLY MEAN THAT! THERE'S JUST ONE THING... WE NEED TO EMPHASIZE THE ***MERCHANDISING*** ASPECT A BIT! LIKE, WHAT IF THE PENGUIN WERE A ***TEENAGE VIGILANTE KILLER PENGUIN?*** WE'VE ALREADY DRAWN UP SOME SKETCHES FOR A SERIES OF ***TOYS...***

GREAT JOB! REALLY, REALLY STRONG WORK! THE ONLY ***PROBLEM*** IS, WE'VE JUST INKED A ***PRODUCT PLACEMENT DEAL***, AND WE NEED TO SHOW THE PENGUIN ***DRINKING A DIET COKE!***

diet Coke

THEN, AT LAST, THE ***FINAL VERSION*** WOULD BE RELEASED...

THIS MODERN WORLD
HEY CITIZENS! WHY DID THE TEENAGE VIGILANTE KILLER PENGUIN CROSS THE ROAD!
WHY THE HELL NOT? NOW GET OUTTA MY WAY-- OR EAT LEAD!

TOM TOMORROW ©'91

THIS MODERN WORLD

by TOM TOMORROW

I HAD THE STRANGEST DREAM LAST NIGHT...

I DREAMT THAT GEORGE BUSH FINALLY GOT A CONSTITUTIONAL AMENDMENT BANNING **FLAG BURNING** PASSED...

AND ALSO THAT, **THANKS** TO HIS **DELIBERATE INACTION** ON THE GLOBAL **WARMING** CRISIS, THE HOLE IN THE OZONE LAYER HAD GROWN TO **DISASTROUS PROPORTIONS**...

TEMPERATURES BEGAN TO RISE SO HIGH THAT OBJECTS LEFT IN THE SUN TOO LONG BEGAN TO SPONTANEOUSLY COMBUST... **FLAGS**, FOR INSTANCE, BEGAN TO BURST INTO FLAME ALL OVER THE COUNTRY...

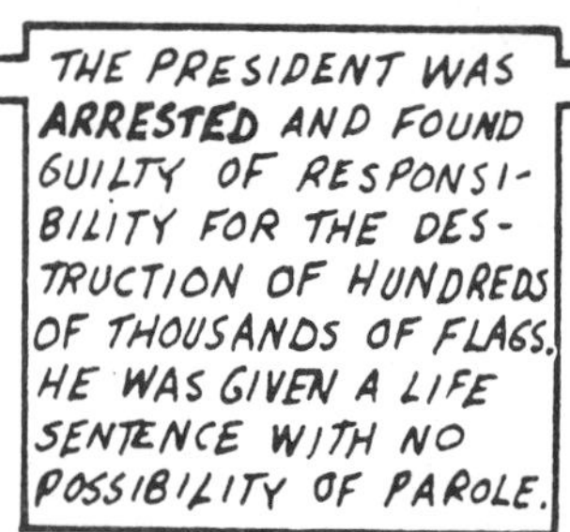
THE PRESIDENT WAS **ARRESTED** AND FOUND GUILTY OF RESPONSIBILITY FOR THE DESTRUCTION OF HUNDREDS OF THOUSANDS OF FLAGS. HE WAS GIVEN A LIFE SENTENCE WITH NO POSSIBILITY OF PAROLE.

WHAT A CRAZY DREAM, HUH?
BOY, IT SURE IS **HOT** TODAY, ISN'T IT?

THIS MODERN WORLD by TOM TOMORROW

AFTER SPENDING ALL DAY SUNDAY READING THE PAPER AND DRINKING COFFEE, BILL AND BETTY REALIZE THEY'VE MADE A TERRIBLE MISTAKE...
OH MY GOSH--IT'S MONDAY MORNING! WE FORGOT TO GO TO BED!
IT'S TIME TO GO TO WORK!
©1990 TOM TOMORROW

THIS MODERN WORLD by TOM TOMORROW

HEY, CITIZENS! IT'S TIME TO TUNE IN TO THE LOCAL NEWS!
GOOD EVENING! IN THE NEWS TONIGHT--GREAT SOCIAL UPHEAVAL IN FAR AWAY PLACES!

WE BEGIN OUR REPORT WITH A FEW QUICK SECONDS OF FOOTAGE FROM THE NETWORK SATELLITE FEED...

NEXT, RATHER THAN SPEND ANY TIME STUDYING AND ATTEMPTING TO COMPREHEND THE UNDERLYING FACTORS INVOLVED, WE'RE JUST GOING TO LET RANDOM PEOPLE ON THE STREET TELL US WHAT THEY THINK ABOUT THE SITUATION!

I THINK IT'S TERRIBLE. REALLY TERRIBLE. SIMPLY AWFUL. ALL THAT UPHEAVAL OVER IN--UH--WHERE IS IT AGAIN?

OF COURSE, THESE OPINIONS ARE BASED ON WHAT LITTLE INFORMATION WE OURSELVES HAVE CONVEYED AND ARE FANTASTICALLY UNINFORMED...
I THINK WE SHOULD NUKE 'EM ALL! THEY'RE ALL CRAZY!

...BUT HEY--WE'RE JUST TRYING TO FILL TIME BETWEEN COMMERCIALS. COMING UP NEXT--A HEARTWARMING STORY ABOUT A LITTLE GIRL AND HER KITTEN.
FIRST THESE MESSAGES.
©1991 TOM TOMORROW

THIS MODERN WORLD by TOM TOMORROW

WHY DRIVE--WHEN YOU CAN TAKE PUBLIC TRANSPORTATION?!

CATCH UP ON YOUR READING!

MAKE INTERESTING NEW FRIENDS!
PSSST! HEY, BUDDY! THE BUS DRIVER IS A CIA ASSASSIN!

MAYBE EVEN GET WHERE YOU'RE GOING!

THIS MODERN WORLD by TOM TOMORROW

WHY, IT'S A NEW LITTLE CONSUMER!
WELL, DON'T YOU WORRY ABOUT A THING, LITTLE FELLA! WE'VE GOT IT ALL PLANNED OUT FOR YOU!
SCHOOL!
ABC 4x5=
A JOB!
RETIREMENT!

THE END!
YOUR LIFE-- YOU'RE JUST ALONG FOR THE RIDE!
©1990 TOM TOMORROW

THIS MODERN WORLD by TOM TOMORROW

HEY, CITIZENS! IT'S TIME FOR ANOTHER WORKING DAY...

7:20 A.M.--ALARM RINGS!

7:40 A.M.--HANDS OFF THAT SNOOZE BUTTON! YOU'VE REALLY GOT TO GET UP!

8:15 A.M.--YOU MADE IT! YOU'RE UP AND DRESSED! NO TIME FOR BREAKFAST, THOUGH--YOU'VE GOT TO RUN!

FROSTED FLAKES

9:05 A.M.--ARRIVE AT OFFICE EXHAUSTED AFTER GRUELLING COMMUTE.

YOU'RE LATE.

9:07 A.M.--DRINK FIRST CUP OF BAD OFFICE COFFEE. HELP YOURSELF--THERE'S PLENTY MORE!

10:37 A.M.--TEDIUM SETS IN. TAKE ANOTHER COFFEE BREAK!

12:00 P.M.--LUNCHTIME! RUN TO THE BANK, THE CLEANERS, AND THE DRUGSTORE--AND MAYBE EVEN GET SOMETHING TO EAT!

1:07 P.M.--WASN'T THAT RELAXING! WELL, BACK TO WORK! HAVE SOME MORE COFFEE!

3:30 P.M.--MID-AFTERNOON DROWSINESS HITS. HANG ON! JUST A FEW MORE HOURS TO GO!

4:45 P.M.--UH OH! THE BOSS GIVES YOU A BIG PROJECT DUE RIGHT AWAY. YOU DON'T MIND WORKING LATE, DO YOU?

8:42 P.M.--HOME AT LAST! NOW YOU CAN DO WHAT YOU WANT--SO TURN ON THAT T.V.!

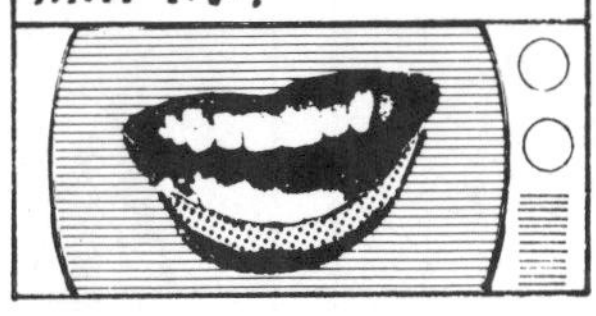

11:33 P.M.--COLLAPSE INTO BED. SUDDENLY YOU'RE WIDE AWAKE. YOU REALLY SHOULDN'T DRINK SO MUCH COFFEE, YOU KNOW.

REPEAT PROCESS FIVE DAYS A WEEK--FOR THE REST OF YOUR LIFE...

THIS MODERN WORLD by TOM TOMORROW

HEY CITIZENS! IT'S TIME FOR THE NEXT ***MUST-SEE MOVIE SENSATION!***

COMING SOON

THE FABULOUS FISH-HEAD FAMILY!

MANY ARTICLES WILL BE WRITTEN! MANY INTERVIEWS WILL BE GIVEN!
TIME
People weekly
FISH-HEADS MAKE A BIG SPLASH
THERE'S SOMETHING FISHY GOING ON!
RollingStone
GLUB! IT'S the FISH-HEADS!

EVERYONE WILL WANT TO BE A PART OF THE EXCITEMENT! LARGE QUANTITIES OF MERCHANDISE WILL BE SOLD!

I'M A FISH-HEAD

IT WILL SEEM MORE IMPORTANT TO MANY PEOPLE THAN THEIR ***OWN LIVES!***

OPENING GROSSES WEREN'T BAD, BUT THEY'VE GOT TO CLEAR AT ***LEAST*** $300 MILLION JUST TO RECOUP THE INITIAL INVESTMENT!
OH I ***DO*** SO HOPE IT WORKS OUT FOR THEM!

THIS MODERN WORLD by TOM TOMORROW

Grrrrrrrr

Grrrrrrrr

Sometimes an artist uses obscurity to hide a lack of underlying substance.
Grrrrrrrr

Grrrrrrrr
©1991 TOM TOMORROW

THIS MODERN WORLD by TOM TOMORROW

SAY, BILL--WE'VE JUST DISCOVERED A MINOR ARITHMETIC ERROR IN OUR RECORDS AND WE NEED YOU TO REFIGURE OUR CORPORATE FINANCIAL RECORDS FOR THE PAST FOUR DECADES... CAN YOU GET THAT TO ME BY FIVE?
SURE, BOSS! NO PROBLEM!
BOY! IT SOUNDS LIKE I'D BETTER TAKE SOME ACCELERATO PLUS™!

ACCELERATO PLUS™ DOUBLES YOUR METABOLIC RATE--SPEEDING UP YOUR SENSE OF SUBJECTIVE TIME SO THAT TEN MINUTES SEEM LIKE TWENTY! ONE HOUR SEEMS LIKE TWO! JUST IMAGINE! YOU'LL BE ABLE TO WORK A SIXTEEN HOUR DAY-- IN JUST EIGHT HOURS!
ACCELERATO PLUS TM

BOY ACCELERATO PLUS™ REALLY WORKED FOR ME I FINISHED THAT WORK FOR THE BOSS AND HAD SO MUCH TIME LEFT OVER THAT I LEARNED A FOREIGN LANGUAGE AND READ THE ENTIRE ENCYCLOPEDIA BRITANNICA AND NOW IDON'TKNOWWHATI'LLDOMAYBESTUDY BRAINSURGERY--
WARNING: ACCELERATO PLUS™ WILL REDUCE YOUR LIFE SPAN BY 50%, BUT JUST THINK OF HOW MUCH YOU'LL GET DONE IN THE MEANTIME...

THIS MODERN WORLD by TOM TOMORROW

HEY, CITIZENS! IT'S TIME FOR THE "VERY SIMPLE MEDICAL ADVICE SHOW," FEATURING YOUR HOST, TEEVEE DOCTOR BOB!
HELLO--IS THE FIRST CALLER THERE?
UH--HELLO? TEEVEE DOCTOR BOB?
YES--GO AHEAD...

DOCTOR BOB--I HAVE A HEADACHE! I DON'T KNOW WHAT TO DO!
A HEADACHE, EH? WELL, WHAT YOU'LL WANT TO DO IS TAKE SOME ASPIRIN!
OH... OKAY!

IS THERE ANOTHER CALLER ON THE LINE?
YES, DOCTOR BOB--I PRICKED MY FINGER ON A SEWING NEEDLE AND IT'S BLEEDING!
OKAY--WHAT YOU NEED TO DO IS WASH THE FINGER AND THEN CAREFULLY APPLY A BAND-AID!
ALL RIGHT... THANK YOU!

OKAY--WE HAVE TIME FOR ONE MORE CALL... CALLER? HELLO?
DOCTOR BOB--I JUST ATE TOO MUCH, AND I FEEL SICK!
HMM... WELL, WHAT YOU SHOULD DO IS TAKE SOME PEPTO-BISMOL!
OKAY! THANKS, DOC!
THAT'S ALL FOR NOW! TUNE IN NEXT TIME FOR MORE SIMPLE ADVICE FROM DR. BOB!
TOM TOMORROW© '91

THIS MODERN WORLD by TOM TOMORROW

HEY BOB! ACCORDING TO THIS NEW POLL, NINETY-THREE PERCENT OF THE AMERICAN PEOPLE BELIEVE THAT POLLS HAVE NO STATISTICAL VALIDITY WHATSOEVER!
WELL, GOSH-- IF THAT'S WHAT EVERYONE THINKS, THEN IT *MUST* BE TRUE!
TOM TOMORROW©91

THIS MODERN WORLD by TOM TOMORROW

HOW THE NEWS WORKS... STEP ONE: SPOKESMAN READS PREPARED STATEMENT DETAILING INFORMATION GOVERNMENT WISHES PUBLIC TO BELIEVE...

YOU SEE, THE PRESIDENT IS MORE POWERFUL THAN A ***LOCOMOTIVE*** AND ABLE TO LEAP TALL BUILDINGS AT A ***SINGLE BOUND***...

STEP TWO: REPORTERS RECORD INFORMATION VERBATIM AND ASK A FEW SUPERFICIAL QUESTIONS WHICH ELICIT EVASIVE ANSWERS...

BUT IS THE PRESIDENT FASTER THAN A ***SPEEDING BULLET***?
WE'VE GOT NO COMMENT AT THIS TIME.

STEP THREE: NEWSPAPERS AND TELEVISION REWRITE GOVERNMENT PRESS RELEASE TO GIVE ILLUSION OF ACTUAL REPORTAGE AND THEN DISSEMINATE INFORMATION...

The New York Times
PRESIDENT STRONGER THAN LOCOMOTIVE
Able To Leap Tall Buildings
Speeding Bullet Question Unanswered

STEP FOUR: PUBLIC ACCEPTS GOVERNMENT PRESS RELEASE AS VERIFIED FACTS UNCOVERED BY A DILIGENT PRESS...

IT'S HARD TO BELIEVE THAT THE PRESIDENT HAS SUCH ***AMAZING POWERS***!
WELL, THEY WOULDN'T ***PRINT*** IT IF IT WASN'T ***TRUE***!
©1991 TOM TOMORROW

THIS MODERN WORLD by TOM TOMORROW

THE PRESIDENT'S COMPELLING STATEMENTS HAVE **ROUSED THE NATION**...

WHY, THIS SADDAM, HE'S WORSE THAN **VLAD THE IMPALER**! HE'S WORSE THAN **BLACKBEARD THE PIRATE**!

UNDEFINED YET IMPORTANT PRINCIPLES ARE AT STAKE--AND MUST BE **DEFENDED**!

A THREAT TO A MONARCHICAL DICTATORSHIP IS A THREAT TO **DEMOCRACY**!
YES! AGGRESSION CANNOT BE TOLERATED, AT LEAST IN THIS ONE PARTICULAR INSTANCE.

EVERYONE'S **PITCHING IN** AND **DOING THEIR PART**--EVEN **FAMOUS MOVIE STARS**!

I AM PLANNING TO GO DOWN THERE, WORK OUT WITH THE TROOPS, SHOW THEM SOME EXERCISES, AND INSPIRE THEM TO **STAY IN SHAPE**!*

*ACTUAL QUOTE--ARNOLD SCHWARTZENEGGER.

YES, THERE'S NOTHING LIKE A **WAR** TO HELP A NATION SET ITS **PRIORITIES**!

ACCORDING TO NEW ESTIMATES, THE S&L BAILOUT WILL COST AMERICANS FIFTY TRILLION DOLLARS **EACH**.
IN MORE **IMPORTANT** NEWS, THE PRESIDENT TODAY DECLARED SADDAM HUSSEIN MORE EVIL THAN **DARTH VADER**!
©1991 TOM TOMORROW

THIS MODERN WORLD by TOM TOMORROW

IT'S TIME FOR THE 11:00 NEWS...
GOOD EVENING! IN THE NEWS TONIGHT-- 100,000 DEMONSTRATORS GATHERED IN THE STREETS OF SAN FRANCISCO TODAY TO PROTEST AGAINST THE WAR IN THE GULF...

100,000 PEOPLE? GOSH, BIFF-- THAT'S COMPLETELY AT ODDS WITH THE CURRENT MEDIA PERCEPTION OF A NATION **STRONGLY UNITED** BEHIND THE ***PRESIDENT***!

THAT'S ***TRUE***, BETTY! THAT'S WHY WE'LL DOWNPLAY THE MAGNITUDE OF THE EVENT BY RUNNING ONLY A FEW BRIEF SECONDS OF FOOTAGE FROM THE DEMONSTRATION...
PEACE NOW
NO WAR
NO BLOOD FOR OIL

...FOLLOWED IMMEDIATELY BY COVERAGE OF FIFTEEN ***PRO-WAR*** DEMONSTRATORS IN WALNUT CREEK-- SUBTLY INDICATING THAT THE TWO EVENTS ARE OF ***EQUAL IMPORTANCE***!
KILL THEM ALL

FINALLY, WE'LL CONCLUDE THE SEGMENT WITH THE LATEST ***NETWORK NEWS POLL*** SHOWING THAT A SOLID 97% OF THE AMERICAN PEOPLE BELIEVE THE ANTI-WAR PROTESTERS ARE ***TRAITOROUS DOGS*** FOR WHOM ***HANGING*** IS ***TOO GOOD***!

COMING UP NEXT: REALLY COOL FOOTAGE OF JET FIGHTERS AND EXPLOSIONS.
FIRST THESE MESSAGES...
TOM TOMORROW

THIS MODERN WORLD by TOM TOMORROW

IT'S TIME FOR ANOTHER *MILITARY PRESS BRIEFING*...
GENERAL--IS THE EARTH *ROUND*?
I'M SORRY--I'M NOT AT LIBERTY TO DISCUSS THAT AT THIS TIME...

GENERAL--IS THE SKY *BLUE*?
AS A MATTER OF POLICY, WE NEVER DISCUSS THE COLOR OF THE SKY.

GENERAL--A FOLLOW-UP, IF I MAY... IS THE GRASS *GREEN*?
PETE-DO WE HAVE ANYTHING ON THAT? NO? I'M SORRY--I'LL HAVE TO GET BACK TO YOU ON THAT.
I'LL TAKE ONE MORE QUESTION.

GENERAL--IS THE POPE *CATHOLIC*?
WELL, I CAN'T REALLY GET INTO THAT AT THIS TIME--BUT I *WILL* SAY THAT THE POPE IS A *VERY RELIGIOUS MAN*.
TUNE IN TOMORROW... FOR EVEN *MORE* INFORMATION!
©1991 TOM TOMORROW

THIS MODERN WORLD

by TOM TOMORROW

LADIES AND GENTLEMEN OF THE MEDIA, I'D LIKE TO THANK YOU ALL FOR ATTENDING THE FIRST ANNUAL "EXCELLENCE IN SHAPING PUBLIC OPINION IN ACCORDANCE WITH WHAT GEORGE BUSH WANTS PEOPLE TO THINK" AWARD CEREMONY!

WE'LL BE PRESENTING EACH OF YOU WITH YOUR VERY OWN "GEORGIE"-- BUT FIRST, I'D LIKE TO EXPRESS MY PERSONAL GRATITUDE FOR THE OUTSTANDING JOB YOU'VE DONE WITH THIS GULF WAR THING!

WE TOLD YOU WHAT TO SAY-- AND YOU SAID IT! NO MISREPRESENTATION OF TRUTH WAS TOO BLATANT FOR YOU!

WE SAID SANCTIONS HAD FAILED--AND YOU CONVINCED THE AMERICAN PEOPLE IT WAS TRUE! WE SAID DIPLOMACY HAD BEEN EXHAUSTED --AND YOU PARROTED OUR ASSERTIONS VERBATIM!

AND TAKE SMART BOMBS -- PLEASE! heh heh. LITTLE JOKE THERE. BUT SERIOUSLY. THANKS TO YOU ALL IN THE MEDIA, HUNDREDS OF THOUSANDS OF DEAD IRAQI CIVILIANS ARE NOTHING MORE THAN "COLLATERAL DAMAGE" TO THE AVERAGE AMERICAN!

SO LET'S GET ON WITH THE SHOW! AFTER YOU RECEIVE YOUR "GEORGIE", BE SURE TO PICK UP YOUR PRESS RELEASE AT THE DOOR-- WE'VE ALREADY WRITTEN THE STORIES YOU'LL WANT TO RUN ABOUT THIS CEREMONY!
PLEASE-DON'T THANK US! WE'RE HAPPY TO MAKE YOUR LIVES EASIER...
©1991 TOM TOMORROW

THIS MODERN WORLD by TOM TOMORROW

IF, WHILE READING A STORY IN THE PAPER--
SOME PEOPLE THINK THAT THE REAGAN TEAM MIGHT HAVE CUT A DEAL WITH THE IRANIANS IN 1980 TO DELAY THE RELEASE OF THE *HOSTAGES*...
BUDGET
ALTERNATIVE AG

--YOU MAKE ALLOWANCES FOR THE FACT THAT POLITICIANS OFTEN *LIE*--

PRESIDENT BUSH SAYS HE DOESN'T EVEN KNOW WHERE IRAN *IS*...

--AND YOU TRY TO READ BETWEEN THE LINES AND DETERMINE WHAT MIGHT HAVE *ACTUALLY* OCCURRED--
HMM... IT *DOES* SEEM SUSPICIOUS THAT THE HOSTAGES WERE RELEASED *MOMENTS* AFTER REAGAN WAS SWORN INTO OFFICE... I *WONDER*...

--WELL--YOU MUST BE SOME KIND OF *CONSPIRACY NUT!* WHAT'S THE *MATTER* WITH YOU? WHY CAN'T YOU JUST BELIEVE WHAT YOU'RE *TOLD*--LIKE A *GOOD AMERICAN*?
NO--THAT'S *CRAZY!* WHAT AM I THINKING? I'M SURE IT WAS JUST A *COINCIDENCE* --LIKE MR. BUSH *SAYS!*
BUDGET
ALTERNATIVE
TOM TOMORROW © '91

THIS MODERN WORLD by TOM TOMORROW

IT'S TIME FOR ANOTHER INSTALLMENT OF "*HOW THE NEWS WORKS*:" THIS WEEK--*EDITORIAL COMMENTARIES*!

STEP ONE: COMMENTATORS FOCUS ATTENTION ON THE MOST SUPERFICIAL ASPECT OF A COMPLEX NEWS STORY...

--AND OF COURSE THE QUESTION ON EVERYONE'S MIND IS, DOES THE REUNIFICATION OF GERMANY MEAN THAT *NAZIS WILL TAKE OVER THE WORLD!?*

STEP TWO: SELF-STYLED EXPERTS SPEND HOURS ON TELEVISION NEWS PROGRAMS DISCUSSING EVERY POSSIBLE RAMIFICATION OF SAID SUPERFICIAL ASPECT...

--AND WE'VE ALSO GOT TO CONSIDER WHAT WE'LL DO IF HITLER'S BRAIN IS IN CYROGENIC STORAGE WAITING TO TELEPATHICALLY CONTROL A REUNIFIED GERMAN ARMY!
YES, THAT'S A VERY GOOD POINT! PERHAPS WHAT'S NEEDED IS MORE FUNDING FOR ANTI-TELEPATHY RESEARCH!

STEP THREE: CITIZENS ACCEPT THE INANITIES UTTERED AS PROBLEMS WITH WHICH THEY NEED BE CONCERNED, AND SIMULTANEOUSLY CONGRATULATE THEMSELVES FOR THEIR KEEN INSIGHT INTO CURRENT EVENTS...

YES, I'M TERRIBLY CONCERNED ABOUT THE PROBLEM OF HITLER'S BRAIN!
ME TOO!

STEP FOUR: WORLD EVENTS ARE COMPLETELY UNAFFECTED BY THE OPINIONS OF COMMENTATORS AND EXPERTS. ANOTHER NEWS STORY CAPTURES EVERYONE'S ATTENTION AND THE ENTIRE PROCESS IS REPEATED...

--BUT IS A CONSTITUTIONAL AMENDMENT *ENOUGH* TO PROTECT THE FLAG? PERHAPS WE NEED TO ABOLISH THE DEMOCRATIC SYSTEM ENTIRELY!
YES--AUTOCRATIC RULE MAY BE THE ONLY SOLUTION!

THIS MODERN WORLD by TOM TOMORROW

WE GET UP IN THE MORNING AND PUT ON OUR BUSINESS SUITS.

WE GO TO OUR VERY IMPORTANT JOBS AND STARE AT COMPUTERS ALL DAY.

AT NIGHT WE GO HOME AND WATCH THE NEWS TO FIND OUT WHAT WE SHOULD THINK ABOUT WORLD EVENTS.
YOU'RE SO PROUD OF OUR RETURNING HEROES.
I'M SO PROUD OF OUR RETURNING HEROES.

ON THE WEEKEND WE CUT LOOSE AND GO WAIT IN LINE TO SEE THE LATEST MUST-SEE MOVIE SPECTACULAR.
ONLY THREE MORE HOURS TO GO!
MAN--THIS IS LIVIN'!

TOM TOMORROW © '91

THIS MODERN WORLD

by TOM TOMORROW

WE'RE PROUD TO BE AMERICANS!
YES! HAVING BEEN BORN IN THE MIDDLE OF THE NORTH AMERICAN LAND MASS HAS ENDOWED US WITH AN INNATE MORAL SUPERIORITY OVER PEOPLE BORN ELSEWHERE!

OUR SENSE OF PRIDE IS, OF COURSE, DEEPENED BY THE UNABASHED SUCCESS OF OUR RECENT MILITARY CONFLICT!
WE KNOW IT WAS AN UNABASHED SUCCESS BECAUSE OUR PRESIDENT SAYS SO!

IT'S A SHAME THAT SOME NAYSAYERS WANT TO MAKE US FEEL BAD BY REMINDING US THAT THE REALITY OF THE WAR'S AFTERMATH IS MUCH LESS CLEAR CUT THAN THE PRESIDENT WOULD HAVE US BELIEVE!
THOSE MALCONTENTS JUST DON'T UNDERSTAND--

--WE DON'T CARE ABOUT REALITY! WE JUST WANT TO FEEL GOOD!
WE'RE ADDICTED TO PATRIOTISM!
GOD BLESS AMERICA! WE'RE NUMBER ONE!
TOM TOMORROW©91

THIS MODERN WORLD

by TOM TOMORROW

CITIZENS WHO WORK FOR LARGE CORPORATIONS GENERALLY DON'T HAVE TO GIVE THEIR HEALTH INSURANCE MUCH *THOUGHT*...

...I HAD A *HEADACHE*...SO I WENT IN FOR *MAGNETIC RESONANCE IMAGING!*

WHAT *HAPPENED?*

THE DOCTOR SAID TO *TAKE SOME ASPIRIN!*

THOSE WHO WORK FOR SMALLER EMPLOYERS PROBABLY HAVE AN *HMO* PLAN THAT CAN BE SOMEWHAT MORE *INCONVENIENT*...

THANK YOU FOR HOLDING, SIR... WE HAVE AN APPOINTMENT AVAILABLE A YEAR FROM NEXT THURSDAY.

SIR? SIR?

THE SELF-EMPLOYED AND UNEMPLOYED MUST EITHER DO WITHOUT INSURANCE *ENTIRELY* OR FACE THE DAUNTING SEARCH FOR INDIVIDUAL COVERAGE...

HAVE YOU BEEN SICK IN THE LAST FIVE YEARS?

WELL, I HAD A *COLD* LAST WINTER...

I'M SORRY-- WE DON'T INSURE PEOPLE WITH A HISTORY OF *ILLNESS*...

THE LUCKY FEW WHO *DO* FIND AN INSURANCE COMPANY WILLING TO WRITE THEM A POLICY MUST THEN FIND A WAY TO *PAY* FOR IT...

WELL...I MAY HAVE TO CUT *BACK* ON A FEW THINGS...LIKE *FOOD*...AND *RENT*...

...BUT AT LEAST I'LL HAVE *INSURANCE*-- IN CASE ANYTHING *BAD* HAPPENS TO ME!

TOM TOMORROW ©'91

THIS MODERN WORLD

by TOM TOMORROW

HEY, THAT'S A PRETTY *MOUTH-WATERING STEAK* YOU'VE GOT THERE!

IT SURE IS!

OF COURSE, YOU'VE GOT TO BE CAREFUL NOT TO *THINK* ABOUT IT TOO *CLOSELY!*

WHAT DO YOU MEAN?

WELL, IT CERTAINLY WOULDN'T DO MUCH FOR YOUR APPETITE TO CONTEMPLATE THE REALITY OF YOUR JUICY STEAK BEING *SLICED* FROM THE BODY OF A *DEAD ANIMAL* --

--A SENTIENT BEING, NOT UNLIKE YOUR OWN BELOVED *DOG* OR *CAT*--

--AND FOR THAT MATTER, NOT SO TERRIBLY UNLIKE *YOU YOURSELF!*

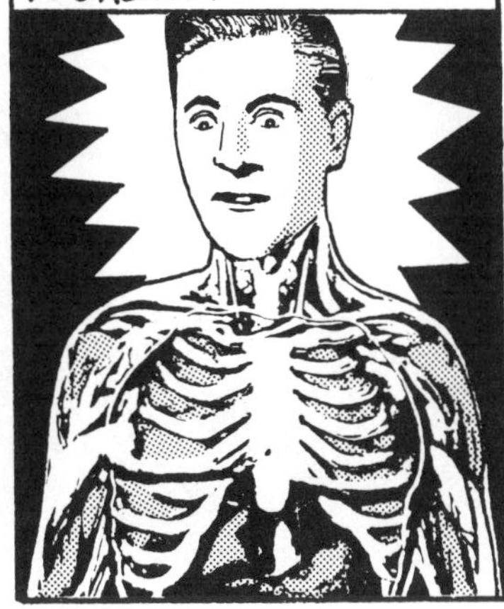

NO, YOU MUSN'T THINK ABOUT THESE THINGS--NOT IF YOU WANT TO BE ABLE TO *EAT* THAT SLAB OF *MEAT* WITHOUT FEELING... *QUEASY*...

WELL--*BON APPETIT!*
GEE... THANKS...
TOM (CARNIVOROUS) TOMORROW ©'91

THIS MODERN WORLD by TOM TOMORROW

THE UNRELENTING OPPRESSION OF "POLITICAL CORRECTNESS" IS THREATENING OUR VERY WAY OF LIFE!

UNDER THE TYRANNY OF *POLITICAL CORRECTNESS*, HATEFUL RACIAL EPITHETS ARE *STRONGLY FROWNED UPON*...

IT'S AN INFRINGEMENT OF MY FREEDOM OF SPEECH!

POLITICALLY CORRECT *THOUGHT POLICE* ATTEMPT TO PROMOTE AN UNDERSTANDING OF CULTURES *OTHER THAN OUR OWN*...

--I'M NOT LISTENING...

FORTUNATELY, THANKS TO THE *HUE AND CRY* RAISED BY *CONSERVATIVE COLUMNISTS*, IT MAY NOT BE TOO LATE TO SAVE THE REPUBLIC FROM THIS *INSIDIOUS MENACE*...

WE'RE JUST DOING OUR JOB...

THIS MODERN WORLD by TOM TOMORROW

HELLO! I'M BOB FRIENDLY-- DIRECTOR OF MARKETING HERE AT **THIS MODERN WORLD**! IN AN EFFORT TO INCREASE THE EXTREMELY LOW **MERCHANDISING POTENTIAL** OF THIS COMIC STRIP, I'VE DECIDED TO INTRODUCE A **HEARTWARMING** AND **LOVABLE** NEW CHARACTER-- **SPARKY**™ THE **WONDER PENGUIN**!
THIS MODERN WORLD

SAY, SPARKY™ --WOULDN'T YOU LIKE TO SHARE SOME OF YOUR **HARMLESS, IRREVERENT WITTICISMS** WITH OUR READERS? SOMETHING ABOUT YOUR **DIET**, PERHAPS? OR THE TROUBLE YOU HAVE GETTING **UP** IN THE MORNING?
GEORGE BUSH IS A **WANKER**.
THIS MODERN WORLD
HEH, HEH... *ahem*... NOW, SPARKY™ -- WE DON'T WANT YOU TO GET TOO **POLITICAL** NOW! AFTER ALL, YOU MIGHT **OFFEND** SOME OF OUR **READERS**!
NOW COME ON-- HOW ABOUT REGALING US WITH SOME OF YOUR EASILY MERCHANDISABLE GREETING-CARD **CATCH PHRASES**?
GEORGE BUSH IS A **WANKER** AND SHOULD BE **IMPEACHED**.

HEH... WELL, HE'S A LITTLE **CANTANKEROUS**, BUT I'M SURE THAT WON'T STOP YOU READERS FROM PURCHASING LARGE QUANTITIES OF SPARKY™ **TIE-IN MERCHANDISING**...
...WILL IT?
DAN QUAYLE IS A WANKER **TOO**.
THIS MODERN WORLD
TOM TOMORROW©'91

THIS MODERN WORLD by TOM TOMORROW

GOSH, WANDA-- I NEVER THOUGHT I'D HAVE A CHANCE TO SEE THE BILL OF RIGHTS WITH MY OWN EYES!
WE HAVE THE ALTRUISM OF A MAJOR TOBACCO COMPANY TO THANK FOR THIS ONCE-IN-A-LIFETIME OPPORTUNITY, BIFF!

THAT'S TRUE! I DON'T KNOW ABOUT YOU, WANDA, BUT INDIVIDUAL LIBERTIES AND CIGARETTE SMOKING ARE NOW INEXTRICABLY LINKED IN MY MIND!

YES! THE FREEDOM TO SMOKE A CIGARETTE IN A CROWDED RESTAURANT IS JUST AS IMPORTANT AS THE FUNDAMENTAL LIBERTIES UPON WHICH OUR SYSTEM OF CONSTITUTIONAL GOVERNMENT IS BASED!

WHY, I THINK I'LL LIGHT ONE UP RIGHT NOW -- FOR DEMOCRACY!
YES... SMOKE...
A PEEK INTO THE DREAMS OF A PHILIP MORRIS EXECUTIVE...
TOM TOMORROW © '91

THIS MODERN WORLD by TOM TOMORROW

GOOD EVENING-- I'M TOM BROKAW. YOU KNOW, OUR CRITICS SOMETIMES CHARGE THAT WE IN THE NEWS MEDIA OVERLOOK CERTAIN IMPORTANT STORIES-- SUCH AS THE *AFRICAN FAMINE CRISIS*...

THEY CLAIM THAT MILLIONS OF FAMINE-STRICKEN AFRICANS MAY *DIE* BECAUSE WE FAILED TO MAKE THE PUBLIC SUFFICIENTLY AWARE OF THEIR DESPERATE NEED FOR IMMEDIATE *AID*...

THESE CRITICS SIMPLY DON'T UNDERSTAND THE BUSINESS OF *NEWS*. YOU SEE, EVERY DAY THERE ARE *HUNDREDS* OF VITALLY IMPORTANT STORIES COMPETING FOR OUR VERY LIMITED TIME AND RESOURCES! WE EXPERIENCED JOURNALISTS MUST OFTEN MAKE *TOUGH DECISIONS*, BALANCING MANY *COMPLEX FACTORS* IN OUR EFFORT TO PRESENT THE MOST WELL-ROUNDED SUMMARY OF THE NEWS *POSSIBLE*!

I HOPE THAT SETTLES *THAT*!
COMING UP NEXT: IN-DEPTH COVERAGE OF MADONNA'S NEW *HAIRSTYLE*.
FIRST THESE MESSAGES.
TOM TOMORROW ©'91

THIS MODERN WORLD

by TOM TOMORROW

A BRIEF GUIDE TO REPUBLICAN ECONOMIC STRATEGY... ***STEP ONE:*** FOR EIGHT YEARS OR SO, ***SPEND MONEY LIKE THERE'S NO TOMORROW!*** DON'T BE SATISFIED UNTIL YOU'VE ACCRUED THE ***LARGEST DEFICIT*** IN ***HUMAN HISTORY!***

STEP TWO: AFTER THE MASSIVE DEBT ACCUMULATED IN STEP ONE LEADS TO AN INEVITABLE ECONOMIC ***DOWNTURN***, CALL A PRESS CONFERENCE AND FIRMLY AND AUTHORITATIVELY ***DENY THE OBVIOUS!***

RECESSION? WHAT RECESSION?
THERE'S NO RECESSION HERE!
THE ECONOMY

STEP THREE: WHEN ALL VARIATIONS ON STEP TWO HAVE BEEN EXHAUSTED, ACKNOWLEDGE THE EXISTENCE OF A PROBLEM--BUT ***BLAME THE VICTIMS!***

THE ECONOMY IS IN TROUBLE BECAUSE CONSUMER SPENDING IS DOWN!
POOR PEOPLE ARE CAUSING THIS RECESSION!

STEP FOUR: FINALLY, SIMPLY DECLARE THAT THE RECESSION IS ***OVER***... AND PRAY THAT THINGS IMPROVE BEFORE THE NEXT ELECTION SO YOU CAN TAKE CREDIT!

THAT'S RIGHT--PROSPERITY NOW REIGNS ACROSS THE LAND!
ANY OTHER QUESTIONS?

THIS MODERN WORLD by TOM TOMORROW

A RECENT NEWS ITEM LINKED **BROOKE SHIELDS** TO THE **BCCI SCANDAL**--

BCCI loans tied to film starring Brooke Shields

ASSOCIATED PRESS

LOS ANGELES — Financial backing on the beleaguered "Brenda Starr" movie starring Brooke Shields and Timothy Dalton has been linked to a Saudi sheik and the Bank of Credit & Commerce International, a newspaper reported Sunday.

Sheik Abdul Aziz al Ibrahim, brother-in-law of Saudi King Fahd, funneled as much as $22.3 million cash and BCCI loan proceeds into the feature film to help Shields get the title role, the Los Angeles Times reported in Sunday's editions.

--WHICH CAN ONLY LEAD ONE TO **WONDER**--

--JUST HOW **FAR** INTO SOCIETY HAVE THE TENTACLES OF THIS CONSPIRACY **EXTENDED**?

...WILL MR. ROGERS PROVE TO HAVE BEEN ON THE TAKE?
CAN YOU SAY SHEIK ABDUL AZIZ AL IBRAHIM?

...HAS YOUR FRIENDLY CORNER GROCER BEEN DABBLING IN THE ARMS TRADE?
CAN I HELP YOU?
pop-tarts

...WHY--WHAT IF YOUR OWN MOTHER HAS BEEN DEEPLY INVOLVED IN A MONEY LAUNDERING SCHEME?
OKAY--WE FUNNEL $7.2 MILLION THROUGH PANAMA--
OOPS--I HAVE TO GO--
HEL-LO DEAR!

THIS MODERN WORLD

by TOM TOMORROW

LIKE MOST CITIZENS, WE'RE ALWAYS CONCERNED ABOUT THE LATEST *TERRIFYING MENACE* TO *DEMOCRACY*!

GRENADA... LIBYA... PANAMA... NICARAGUA... IRAQ...
NO MATTER HOW IMPLAUSIBLE THE THREAT THEY POSE MAY *SEEM*, IF OUR LEADERS TELL US TO *FEAR* THEM-- WE *DO*!

BUT NO ONE HAS TOLD US WHAT TO BE AFRAID OF SINCE WE OBLITERATED *IRAQ*!
AND WITHOUT AN EXTERNAL THREAT TO OCCUPY OUR ATTENTION, WE FIND OURSELVES DWELLING ON MATTERS SUCH AS THE *RECESSION*... THE *HOMELESS*... THE NATION'S *CRUMBLING INFRASTRUCTURE* ...DILEMMAS FOR WHICH THERE ARE NO *EASY MILITARY SOLUTIONS*!

WE NEED SOMETHING *NEW* TO *WORRY ABOUT*--
--TO TAKE OUR MINDS OFF OUR *PROBLEMS*!
TOM TOMORROW©'91

THIS MODERN WORLD by TOM TOMORROW

GOOD EVENING AND WELCOME TO THE **MACNEIL-LEHRER NEWS HOUR!** I'M ROBERT MACNEIL...

...AND I'M JIM LEHRER. YOU KNOW, ROBERT, I JUST CAN'T GET OVER THE FACT THAT SO MANY OF OUR VIEWERS ARE LIBERALS WHO WATCH OUR SHOW FOR THE **BALANCED COVERAGE** THEY BELIEVE IT PROVIDES...

THAT **IS** AMUSING, JIM... PARTICULARLY SINCE THE BULK OF OUR SHOW IS SO OFTEN DEVOTED TO EXPLAINING WHAT **CONSERVATIVE REPUBLICANS** THINK OF WORLD EVENTS...

...OUR DEBATES ARE USUALLY CONFINED TO THE DIFFERENCES OF OPINION BETWEEN **MODERATE** AND **HARD LINE RIGHT-WINGERS**...

...AND MUCH OF OUR FUNDING COMES FROM **MULTINATIONAL CORPORATIONS** AND **DEFENSE CONTRACTORS!**

HEE, HEE! MAYBE AFTER THEY WATCH THE **NEWS HOUR** TONIGHT, THOSE VIEWERS CAN GO OUT FOR A **GOURMET MEAL... AT McDONALDS!**
ahem! IN THE **NEWS** TONIGHT...
TOM TOMORROW ©'91

THIS MODERN WORLD by TOM TOMORROW

OUR INTREPID CORRESPONDENT SPARKY™ THE WONDER PENGUIN IS ON SPECIAL ASSIGNMENT THIS WEEK...IN WASHINGTON!
EXCUSE ME--MR. PRESIDENT? GEORGE? YOO HOO!
WAKE UP, YOU WANKER!
ZZZZZZZ*
HUH? WHA-?
TAP TAP

LISTEN, I'VE BEEN WONDERING...WHY IS IT THAT THE CIA--INTO WHICH TENS OF MILLIONS OF DOLLARS ARE POURED EACH YEAR--HAS BEEN CAUGHT COMPLETELY OFF GUARD BY MANY OF THE MAJOR POLITICAL DEVELOPMENTS OF THE LAST DECADE OR SO...INCLUDING THE RECENT SOVIET UPHEAVAL, THE IRAQI INVASION OF KUWAIT, THE COLLAPSE OF THE BERLIN WALL, AND THE IRANIAN REVOLUTION?
?

IS IT POSSIBLY BECAUSE THEY'VE JUST BEEN TOO DAMNED BUSY? TOO BUSY PROPPING UP CORRUPT LATIN AMERICAN DICTATORSHIPS, WAGING UNDECLARED WARS AGAINST IMPOVERISHED THIRD WORLD COUNTRIES, RUNNING GUNS AND SMUGGLING DRUGS, CAVORTING WITH TERRORISTS AND GANGSTERS, AND GENERALLY ENGAGING IN GOD ONLY KNOWS WHAT OTHER UNCONSTITUTIONAL AND ILLEGAL COVERT ACTIVITIES?
GOSH--YOU'RE NOWHERE NEAR AS ENDEARING AS GARFIELD OR SNOOPY, ARE YOU?
I SUPPOSE NOT. SAY, I WAS ALSO WONDERING HOW YOU PLAN TO DEAL WITH THE HUMILIATING DISGRACE WHICH WILL ENSUE WHEN YOUR ROLE IN THE IRAN-CONTRA/OCTOBER SURPRISE SCANDAL IS INEVITABLY REVEALED...
TOM TOMORROW © '91

THIS MODERN WORLD by TOM TOMORROW

HOW THE **ADVERTISING INDUSTRY** WORKS... **STEP ONE:** AGENCY WOOS A POTENTIAL CLIENT BY DEMONSTRATING THE DEPTH OF THEIR **DEVOTION** TO HIS **PRODUCT**...

YES, MR. TOMORROW-- WE ALL SIMPLY **LOVE** YOUR COMIC STRIP!
AND WE THINK A SUGAR-COATED SNACK PRODUCT IN THE SHAPE OF YOUR RECURRENT CHARACTER "SPARKY™ THE WONDER PENGUIN" IS A **TERRIFIC** IDEA!
SPARKY CHIPS

STEP TWO: ONCE THE CLIENT IS SECURED, THE AGENCY'S "CREATIVES" PROCEED TO DEVELOP AN AD CAMPAIGN-- WITH THE INTENSITY AND SELF-IMPORTANCE OF WORLD LEADERS NEGOTIATING A NUCLEAR TREATY...

'EAT **SPARKY CHIPS** OR YOU'RE A **DIP**'-- NO--
'YOU'LL **FLIP** FOR SPARKY CHIPS'-- NO--NO--
THINK! WE'VE GOT TO **THINK!**

STEP THREE: IN ORDER TO GAUGE PROBABLE CONSUMER REACTION TO THEIR IDEAS, THE AGENCY HOLDS **FOCUS GROUPS**--CONSISTING OF CAREFULLY-CHOSEN SUBJECTS WHO HAVE LIED THROUGH THEIR TEETH IN ORDER TO QUALIFY FOR THE PAYING SESSION...

SO-- YOU ALL LOVE SUGAR-COATED SNACK PRODUCTS?
YOU BET!
$
CAN'T GET ENOUGH OF 'EM!
$

STEP FOUR: STEPS TWO AND THREE ARE REPEATED **AD INFINITUM**... UNTIL THE "CREATIVES" HAVE SPENT SO MUCH TIME ON THE PROJECT THAT THEY ARE **COMPLETELY INCAPABLE** OF OBJECTIVELY JUDGING THE END RESULT...

♫ LOVE TO CHEW THOSE SPARKY CHIPS WITH THE TEETH BEHIND MY LIPS! ♫
IT'S-- IT'S-- **BRILLIANT**...

THIS MODERN WORLD by TOM TOMORROW

ONE DAY, WHILE WATCHING THE NEWS, FRED WAS SUDDENLY BESET BY *STRANGE DOUBTS*...

GOSH... PRESIDENT BUSH IS ***REALLY PUSHING*** FOR A FREE TRADE AGREEMENT WITH MEXICO...

IS IT POSSIBLE THAT THE PRES-IDENT IS MORE CONCERNED WITH GIVING CORPORA-TIONS ACCESS TO CHEAP LABOR ACROSS THE BOR-DER THAN WITH THE PLIGHT OF THE AMERICAN WORKER?

GOOD LORD... IS IT FURTHER POSSIBLE THAT I'VE BEEN ***SUCKERED*** BY SUCH NON-ISSUES AS ***FLAG BURNING*** AND ***WILLIE HOR-TON*** INTO SUPPORT-ING AN ADMINIS-TRATION WITH ONE SIMPLE ***HIDDEN AGENDA***-- HELPING THE RICH GET ***RICH-ER*** AT THE REST OF THE COUNTRY'S ***EXPENSE?***

FORTUNATELY FOR FRED'S PEACE OF MIND, A WELL-STAGED PHOTO OP CAME ON THE SCREEN AND DISTRACTED HIM...
HEY! THERE'S SCHWARZKOPF VIS-ITING A FLAG FACTORY!
...WHAT WAS I JUST THINKING ABOUT..?
...OH WELL...
TOM TOMORROW© '91

THIS MODERN WORLD by TOM TOMORROW

HEY, CITIZENS! IT'S TIME FOR YET ANOTHER EDITION OF *"HOW THE NEWS WORKS"*..

STEP ONE: THE PRESIDENT DESCRIBES, IN VAGUE AND GENERAL TERMS, THE BENEFITS OF A ***FREE TRADE AGREEMENT*** WITH ***MEXICO***.

FREE ENTERPRISE! GROWTH! BLAH! BLAH! BLAH!

STEP TWO: AN ECONOMIST IS TROTTED OUT TO EXPLAIN HOW THROWING THOUSANDS OF PEOPLE OUT OF WORK WILL BE ***GOOD*** FOR THE ***ECONOMY***.

YOU SEE, ONCE BUSINESSES ARE FREE TO MOVE OPERATIONS TO ***MEXICO***...

...THEY WILL NO LONGER BE FORCED TO PAY EXHORBITANT WAGES TO AMERICAN WORKERS! CORPORATE PROFITS WILL ***SOAR!*** THE ECONOMY WILL ***TURN AROUND!*** THE RECESSION WILL ***END!***

STEP THREE: POSSIBLY-- JUST ***POSSIBLY***-- A REPORTER WILL ASK THE OBVIOUS QUESTION...

...BUT--WHAT WILL HAPPEN TO ALL THE WORKERS WHO LOSE THEIR ***JOBS?***
OH, NO PROBLEM--THEY'LL BE ***RETRAINED!***

STEP FOUR: DOUBTS THUS ASSUAGED BY GLIB REASSURANCES, THE MAINSTREAM NEWS MEDIA FALLS DUTIFULLY INTO LINE...

--AND AFTER ALL-- WHAT'S GOOD FOR ***BUSINESS*** IS GOOD FOR ***AMERICA!***

STEP FIVE: THE PRESIDENT EVENTUALLY GETS HIS WAY. DISPLACED WORKERS ARE RETRAINED AND SETTLE INTO FULFILLING NEW CAREERS.

YOU WANT ***FRIES*** WITH THAT?
FUN
MEAL®
TOM TOMORROW © '91

THIS MODERN WORLD by TOM TOMORROW

SAY--WHAT'S **SPARKY™** THE **WONDER PENGUIN** UP TO **THIS** WEEK?

PSST--GEORGE--IT'S ME--**BILL CASEY!**

LISTEN, I'VE BEEN **THINKING**--I THINK YOU SHOULD **COME CLEAN** TO THE AMERICAN PEOPLE AND ADMIT THE DEPTH OF YOUR INVOLVEMENT IN THE **OCTOBER SURPRISE**.

ZZZZ...BILL...?

BILL...I CAN'T DO THAT...THEY'D IMPEACH ME...
MY GOD...WHAT WE DID...WAS TREASON...
...BILL...? AREN'T YOU...DEAD--?

AUGH!

GEORGE--DID YOU HAVE ANOTHER DREAM ABOUT THAT PENGUIN?
BUT BAR--HE'S REAL! HE WAS RIGHT HERE!
GEORGE, I'M WORRIED ABOUT YOU.

THIS MODERN WORLD by TOM TOMORROW

DURING THE EIGHTIES, GOVERNMENT DE-REGULATED CORPORATIONS AND SLASHED TAXES ON THE WEALTHY!
THAT'S TRUE!

BY MAKING THE RICH RICHER, IT WAS PRESUMED THAT EVERYONE WOULD BENEFIT!
A RISING TIDE LIFTS ALL BOATS!

BUT NOW WE FIND OURSELVES DEEP IN A RECESSION, WITH UNEMPLOYMENT RAM-PANT!
THERE'S OBVIOUSLY ONLY ONE SOLUTION--

--MORE DEREGULATION AND UPPER INCOME TAX CUTS!
IF THE POOR DON'T LIKE IT, LET 'EM BUY THEIR OWN SENATORS!

THIS MODERN WORLD

by TOM TOMORROW

NOW, ABOUT EXTENDING THESE UNEMPLOYMENT BENEFITS--I'M **AGAINST** IT! GOVERNMENT HANDOUTS--DON'T **BELIEVE** IN 'EM! SELF-RELIANCE--**THAT'S** THE SOLUTION!
AH, MR. PRESIDENT--

--SIR, SINCE THE WHITE HOUSE PRESS CORPS IS COMPRISED OF A BUNCH OF **WEENIES** AFRAID OF OFFENDING YOU AND POSSIBLY LOSING THEIR POSITIONS OF **PRIVILEGE**, I GUESS **I'LL** HAVE TO ASK THE OBVIOUS QUESTION--

--IF YOU ARE UNTROUBLED BY A $200 BILLION S&L BAILOUT AND A $70 BILLION FDIC BAILOUT--BOTH NECESSITATED BY THE **GREED** AND **MISMANAGEMENT** OF YOUR REPUBLICAN **CRONIES**--
--**WHY** DO YOU BALK AT SPENDING A **FRACTION** OF THAT TO HELP **AMERICANS IN NEED**?

COULD IT BE THAT YOU **DO** BELIEVE IN GOVERNMENT HANDOUTS--BUT ONLY FOR THE **RICH**?!
WELL, I--UH--ahem!
WHAT PAPER DID YOU SAY YOU'RE WITH?
©91 TOM TOMORROW

THIS MODERN WORLD by TOM TOMORROW

HEY CITIZENS! THE FASHION WORD FOR **FALL** IS... **PLAID**!
Fashion Extra
Guy Anxiety: His 8 Greatest Love Fears
basics

WHAT IS IT THAT MAKES PLAID **SO DARNED SPECIAL**? IS IT THE **DARING SWEEP** OF THE **VERTICAL LINES**? THE **TRADITIONAL SECURITY** OF THE **HORIZONTAL LINES**?

...OR IS IT THE SENSE OF **LIMITLESS POSSIBILITY** SUGGESTED BY THE INTERSECTION OF **BOTH** ELEMENTS?
WELL-- **WE** CERTAINLY DON'T PRETEND TO HAVE THE ANSWER... BUT WE KNOW **ONE** THING FOR SURE--

--IF YOU DON'T WEAR **PLAID** THIS FALL... NO ONE WILL **LIKE** YOU!
GEEZ-- JUST **LOOK** AT HER!
WHY DOESN'T SHE **GET WITH IT**?

THIS MODERN WORLD by TOM TOMORROW

SAY, BIFF--WHAT HAVE YOU GOT THERE?
WHY, ANOTHER THOUGHT-PROVOKING ISSUE OF **NEWSWEEK MAGAZINE**, WANDA!
Newsweek
SHOULD WOMEN FIGHT TO KILL?

NEWSWEEK ALWAYS HELPS ME UNDERSTAND THE **ISSUES** OF THE DAY! FOR INSTANCE, THIS WEEK'S COVER STORY EXAMINES THE QUESTION OF WHETHER WOMEN IN THE MILITARY SHOULD FIGHT TO **KILL**!
HMM...
Newsweek
SHOULD WOMEN FIGHT TO KILL?

GOSH, BIFF--DO THEY QUESTION WHETHER **MEN** SHOULD FIGHT TO KILL? WHETHER **ANYONE** SHOULD? DO THEY QUESTION THE UNDERLYING ASSUMPTION PREVALENT IN OUR SOCIETY THAT KILLING A LARGE NUMBER OF PEOPLE OF A GIVEN NATIONALITY IS A **JUSTIFIABLE** AND **MORAL ACT** AS LONG AS OUR PRESIDENT HAS USED SOME TRANSPARENT EXCUSE TO DECLARE THEM **'ENEMIES'**?

WELL--**NO!** OF **COURSE** NOT!
THIS IS **NEWSWEEK MAGAZINE**, WANDA--NOT SOME WEIRDO LEFTIST **PROPAGANDA SHEET**!
YES, OF COURSE--I DON'T KNOW WHAT I COULD HAVE BEEN **THINKING**...
Newsweek
TOM TOMORROW©91

THIS MODERN WORLD by TOM TOMORROW

GOSH, SPARKY™ --ISN'T IT **GREAT** WHEN THE **BLUE ANGELS** COME TO TOWN?

SURE, BOB-- WHAT COULD BE MORE EXCITING THAN WATCHING A TEAM OF STUNT-FLYING **FIGHTER JETS** ZOOM-ING WINGTIP-TO-WINGTIP OVER A DENSELY POPULATED **MAJOR MET-ROPOLITAN AREA**--

--WITH A MARGIN OF ERROR SO SLIM THAT **ONE MINOR PILOT MISCALCULA-TION** COULD RESULT IN THE DESTRUC-TION OF **GOD ONLY KNOWS** HOW MANY CITY BLOCKS!

YOU'RE NOT REALLY INTO THE **SPIRIT** OF THIS, ARE YOU, SPARKY™?
DON'T BE SILLY. I ENJOY ARRO-GANT DISREGARD FOR CIVILIAN SAFETY AS MUCH AS THE NEXT PENGUIN.

TOM TOMORROW © '91

THIS MODERN WORLD by TOM TOMORROW

THANK YOU! THANK YOU!
CLAP
CLAP
CLAP

FOR MY NEXT AMAZING FEAT OF PRES-TIDIGITATION I WILL MAKE THE ARMS RACE DISAPPEAR--

--WITHOUT, INCREDIBLY ENOUGH--
POOF!

--REDUCING THE MILITARY BUD-GET IN THE LEAST!
THANK YOU! THANK YOU!
CLAP
CLAP
CLAP
TRILLIONS SPENT
©'91 TOM TOMORROW

THIS MODERN WORLD by TOM TOMORROW

OUR INTREPID CORRESPONDENT **SPARKY™** IS IN **LOUISIANA** THIS WEEK...

OKAY--LET ME SEE IF I'VE GOT THIS STRAIGHT--AFRICAN-AMERICANS WERE BROUGHT TO THIS COUNTRY AS **SLAVES**...

BEER DRINKER

AFRI-CAN AMUR-ICANS?

HE MEANS **NEGRAS**!

...IN THE INTERVENING YEARS, THEY HAVE LARGELY BEEN FORCED BY ECONOMIC AND SOCIAL FACTORS TO LIVE IN THE VIR-TUAL CONTAINMENT CAMPS OF THE INNER CITIES--WHERE OPPORTUNITIES ARE LIMITED AT **BEST**...
BEER DRINKER
DUKE

...AND SINCE DAVID DUKE'S NEAR WIN HERE IN LOUISIANA PROVES RACISM IS ALIVE AND WELL IN TODAY'S SOCIETY, AN AFRICAN-AMERICAN CAN HARDLY BE BLAMED FOR SUSPECTING THAT THE ODDS MIGHT BE AGAINST HIM OR HER IN THE **JOB MARKET**...
BEER DRINKER

...AND YET, YOU GUYS CONSIDER AFFIRM-ATIVE ACTION UNJUST TO **YOU?!**
HELL YES! IT AIN'T **FAIR** IF WE DON'T GET PREFERENTIAL TREATMENT FOR BEIN' **WHITE**!
HEY BILLY BOB--YOU NOTICE THIS BIRD'S HALF **BLACK?**
BEER DRINKER
TOM TOMORROW©'91

THIS MODERN WORLD by TOM TOMORROW

SWAMI SPARKY™ HAS A FEW PREDICTIONS FOR THE 1992 PRESIDENTIAL CAMPAIGN...
I SEE... THE DEMOCRATS HOPING TO APPEAL TO EVERYONE BY OFFENDING NO ONE...
THEY CHOOSE A SAFE, BLAND, AND UTTERLY BORING CANDIDATE...

PRESIDENT BUSH, MEANWHILE, PROPOSES A SERIES OF "QUICK FIX" ECONOMIC SOLUTIONS WHICH IGNORE LONG TERM PROBLEMS BUT, MORE IMPORTANTLY, BOOST HIS APPROVAL RATINGS...
...AND SO I HAVE DECIDED TO GIVE EVERY AMERICAN CITIZEN A NEW CAR!
ALL RIGHT!

...PERHAPS HE EVEN INVOLVES THE U.S. IN ANOTHER SHORT, WINNABLE WAR AGAINST AN EASILY VILIFIED ENEMY SUCH AS LIBYA OR CUBA, SETTING OFF A BRIEF BUT WELL-TIMED SPASM OF PATRIOTIC FUROR...
THIS IS NO TIME FOR PARTISAN DEBATE!
WE'VE GOT TO STAND BEHIND OUR PRESIDENT!
NOVEMBER

IN ANY CASE, BUSH IS RE-ELECTED ON NOV. 4 BY A MAJORITY OF THE THOUSAND OR SO AMERICANS WHO ACTUALLY BOTHER TO VOTE...
IT'S A CLEAR MANDATE!
The New York Times.
BUSH WINS BY 15 VOTES
TOM TOMORROW©'92--1-7-92--HOPE I'M WRONG...

THIS MODERN WORLD by TOM TOMORROW

FROM THE MYTH OF THE OCTOBER SURPRISE TO THE TWISTED TRUTH OF JFK ...I'M CERTAINLY THANKFUL THAT NEWSWEEK MAGAZINE DOESN'T TOLERATE ANY NONSENSE FROM THESE CONSPIRACY NUTS!
Newsweek
TREASON
MYTH
Newsweek
The Twisted Truth of 'JFK'

SURE, BIFF-- THANK HEAVENS THEY'RE LEVEL-HEADED ENOUGH TO DISREGARD THE PARANOID NOTION THAT THE BUSINESS OF POLITICS MAY TAKE PLACE MORE OFTEN BEHIND CLOSED DOORS THAN AT STAGED PHOTO OPS...
this is tomorrow
INSIDE

...AND RESPONSIBLE ENOUGH NOT TO FALL FOR THE WACKO THEORY THAT THE PRACTITIONERS OF POLITICS MAY NOT ALWAYS BE OF THE HIGHEST MORAL CALIBER--AND MAY, ON OCCASION, ACTUALLY ABUSE THEIR AUTHORITY!
whitechapel art gallery
IN$IDE

YES, NEWSWEEK MAGAZINE ALLOWS ME TO SLEEP BETTER AT NIGHT-- KNOWING THE STATUS QUO IS SAFE FOR ANOTHER WEEK!
YOU'RE BEING SARCASTIC AGAIN, AREN'T YOU, SPARKY™?
CAN'T SLIP ANYTHING PAST YOU, CAN I, BIFF?
this is tomorrow
TOM TOMORROW© '92

THIS MODERN WORLD by TOM TOMORROW

GOSH, BETTY-- WEREN'T THE THOMAS/HILL HEARINGS SHOCKING?
THEY SURE WERE, BIFF!

I JUST CAN'T BELIEVE THAT SOMEONE WAS SO UNSCRUPULOUS AS TO LEAK ANITA HILL'S CHARGES TO THE PRESS...
WAIT A MINUTE...

...THE LEAK OF INFORMATION IS WHAT YOU FOUND SHOCKING?
OF COURSE! HOW ON EARTH CAN WE EXPECT OUR ELECTED OFFICIALS TO RUN OUR DEMOCRACY--

--IF THEY AREN'T ALLOWED TO DO SO IN SECRECY?
YES--HOW TERRIBLY INCONVENIENT FOR THEM...
TOM TOMORROW©91

THIS MODERN WORLD by TOM TOMORROW

I WAS IN MY OFFICE FINISHING LUNCH--A SHOT OF WHISKEY AND A PLATE OF LEFTOVER FISH ENTRAILS --WHEN ***SHE*** WALKED THROUGH THE DOOR...

SPARKY
T.W.
PENGUIN
PRIVATE
EYE

HER SKIN WAS A PALE, SICKLY ***GREEN*** AND THERE WAS A DISTANT LOOK IN HER EYES... IT WAS OBVIOUS THAT SHE'D SEEN BETTER DAYS...

I NEED YOUR HELP, MR. PENGUIN--I'VE GOT A THREE TRILLION DOLLAR DEFICIT AND I DON'T KNOW HOW IT HAPPENED...

I TOLD HER I'D TAKE THE CASE... I ALREADY KNEW WHO I NEEDED TO TALK TO ***FIRST...***

HE WAS AN OLD GEEZER WHO COULD BARELY REMEMBER HIS ***NAME...*** BUT LOCKED AWAY SOMEWHERE IN THE PATHETIC RECESSES OF HIS ENFEEBLED MIND WERE THE ***ANSWERS*** I ***NEEDED...***

WHERE DID THE MONEY GO? TALK, DAMN YOU!
THE MONEY...

OH YES--THE MONEY... WHY...WE SPENT IT--ON INVISIBLE PLANES--AND SPACE UMBRELLAS--AND TAX SUBSIDIES FOR MILLIONAIRES...
...AND IF WE DIDN'T HAVE ENOUGH... WE JUST PRINTED MORE!

MOST OF WHAT HE SAID WAS INDECIPHERABLE ***LUNACY***, BUT ***ONE*** THING SEEMED CLEAR--I'D STUMBLED ONTO THE BIGGEST ***FUNNY MONEY*** SCAM IN ***HISTORY...*** (CONT'D NEXT WEEK!)

TOM TOMORROW ©92

THIS MODERN WORLD

by TOM TOMORROW

(CONT'D) I'D BEEN HIRED BY A GREEN DAME WHO CALLED HERSELF LADY LIBERTY TO FIND OUT WHY HER BOOKS HAD COME UP $3 TRILLION SHORT..
THE TRAIL LED ME TO THE SLEAZY SIDE OF TOWN... THE DARK UNDERBELLY OF THE FREE MARKET ECONOMY, WHERE PEOPLE ARE THE COMMODITY...
TOPLESS
LOVE ACT
NUDE GIRLS

...FOR IT WAS THERE I KNEW I'D BE LIKELY TO FIND THE PARTICULAR LOWLIFE I SOUGHT-- A U.S. CONGRESSMAN...
HEY, SUGAR-- LOOKIN' FOR A DATE?
PSSST-- LEGISLATION-- CHEAP!
WEED-- DOSES--
INFLUENCE!

I CORNERED ONE AND GOT HIS ATTENTION WITH A SAWBUCK...
MY CLIENT'S BEEN SADDLED WITH A $3 TRILLION DEFICIT! WHY DIDN'T YOU RE-REGULATE THE S&L'S? OR CUT THE BLOATED PENTAGON BUDGET? WHY DIDN'T YOU DO SOMETHING?
QUITE SIMPLY, MR. PENGUIN, I WAS TOO BUSY RAISING MONEY FOR MY RE-ELECTION CAMPAIGN!

NOW, IF YOU'LL EXCUSE ME, SIR, THE NIGHT IS YOUNG...
CAN I OFFER YOU SOME COMFORTING PLATITUDES ABOUT GOD, FAMILY, AND LOVE OF COUNTRY TO SEE YOU ON YOUR WAY?
NO THANKS-- I JUST ATE...
NEXT WEEK: MR. BIG!
TOM TOMORROW ©92

THIS MODERN WORLD by TOM TOMORROW

(CONT'D) I'D BEEN HIRED TO TRACK DOWN A $3 TRILLION DEFICIT... AND MY INVESTIGATION HAD FINALLY LED ME TO MR. BIG...
I HEAR YOU BEEN ASKIN' A LOT OF QUESTIONS AROUND TOWN, PENGUIN...
I WANT TO KNOW WHERE THE MONEY WENT, GEORGE...

WHAT MONEY? THERE AIN'T NO PROBLEM WITH MONEY! TH' RACKETS ARE GONNA TURN AROUND ANY DAY NOW AND EVERYTHING'LL BE JUST FINE! YOU SAVVY?
SURE GEORGE...
I SAVVIED THAT HE WAS COMPLETELY OUT OF TOUCH WITH REALITY... FORTUNATELY, I HAD ONE LAST LEAD TO FOLLOW...

I HEADED NEXT FOR THE COMFORTABLE SUBURBAN HOME OF MR. AND MRS. JOHN Q. PUBLIC...
WE DON'T KNOW WHAT YOU'RE TALKIN' ABOUT, PENGUIN!
OH JOHN--CAN'T YOU SEE IT'S TOO LATE? IT'S TIME TO ADMIT THE UGLY TRUTH--
WE DID IT, MR. PENGUIN--WE VOTED REPUBLICAN IN THE LAST THREE ELECTIONS!
TOM TOMORROW©92

YOU SEE, WE KNEW IT WAS WRONG--BUT WE WANTED TO BELIEVE THAT A DEFICIT-FINANCED ECONOMIC BOOM COULD BE SUSTAINED INDEFINITELY!
SHUT UP, JANE!
SORRY, JOHN--THE JIG IS UP... AND THE BILL HAS COME DUE!
AMOUNT DUE: $3,000,0
YEAH, THE BILL HAD COME DUE, ALL RIGHT... THE TROUBLE WAS, WE WERE ALL GOING TO BE PAYING IT... FOR A LONG, LONG TIME...
END?

THIS MODERN WORLD by TOM TOMORROW

WE RECENTLY RECEIVED A LETTER HERE AT **THIS MODERN WORLD** FROM A READER WHO TOOK EXCEPTION TO OUR '**OVER-SIMPLIFICATION**' IN BLAMING THE S&L FIASCO ON THE **REPUBLICANS**-- AND AFTER A GREAT DEAL OF SOUL-SEARCHING WE'VE REALIZED HE'S **RIGHT**!
THIS MODERN WORLD
THIS MAY ONLY BE A FOUR-PANEL CARTOON--BUT BY GOSH WE'RE NOT GOING TO MAKE ANY MORE **CHEAP GENERALIZATIONS** WITHOUT THOROUGHLY EXAMINING **ALL SIDES** OF THE ISSUE!
WE'RE GOING TO START THIS WEEK WITH A MORE CAREFUL, **BALANCED** LOOK AT THE S&L BAILOUT!

...AND THEREFORE IT SHOULD BE OBVIOUS THAT THE CRISIS IS ENTIRELY THE FAULT OF **REPUBLICAN GREEDHEADS FROM HELL**!
YOUR LOGIC IS **IRREFUTABLE**, SPARKY™!
NEXT WEEK: **THIS MODERN WORLD** EXAMINES THE **MEANING** OF **EXISTENCE**!
TOM TOMORROW ©91

THIS MODERN WORLD by TOM TOMORROW

IN THIS MODERN WORLD, MANY THINGS WHICH WERE ONCE CONSIDERED THE ***BIRTHRIGHT*** OF EVERY AMERICAN ARE INCREASINGLY ***DIFF-ICULT*** TO ACHIEVE...

BANK ACCOUNT
GOOD SALARY
FINE CAR
A NICE HOME

MIDDLE-CLASS CITIZENS ARE HAVING TROUBLE MEETING THE PAYMENTS ON THEIR MANY POSSESSIONS--AND IN SOME CASES ARE AC-TUALLY FORCED TO DO ***WITHOUT*** THINGS THEY ***WANT!***

LIFE JUST DOESN'T SEEM COMPLETE WITHOUT A HIGH-DEFINITION STEREO-PHONIC COMBINA-TION TELEVISION/ DISHWASHER...

MANY COLLEGE GRADUATES--EVEN ***BUSINESS STUDENTS***--ARE UNABLE TO FIND HIGH-PAYING JOBS IMMEDIATELY UPON GRADUATION AND MUST ***POSTPONE*** THEIR DREAMS OF ACQUISITION...

BUT--BUT-- I'VE GOT AN M.B.A.!
JOB OPPORTUNITIES

IT JUST DOESN'T SEEM ***FAIR***, BUT HARD TIMES ARE FORCING MIDDLE-CLASS AMER-ICANS TO LOWER THEIR ***EXPECTATIONS*** AND LIVE WITH ***LESS***...

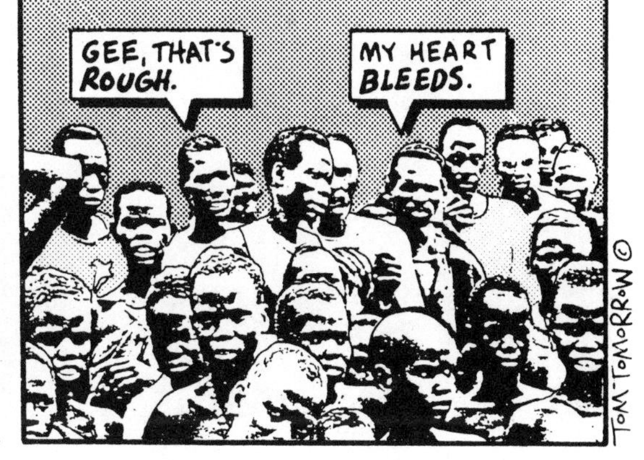
GEE, THAT'S ROUGH.
MY HEART BLEEDS.
TOM TOMORROW ©

THIS MODERN WORLD by TOM TOMORROW

EVERY DAY, IN WORKPLACES AROUND THE COUNTRY, CITIZENS FIND RESPITE FROM THE TEDIUM OF THEIR JOBS BY DISCUSSING THE **ONE SUBJECT** THAT FASCINATES US **ALL**--**FAMOUS MOVIE STARS**!

I HEARD THAT THE MOVIE COMPANY GAVE ARNOLD A LEAR JET!
WELL--HE DESERVES IT! HE WORKS HARD!

YES, **MOVIE STARS**! THEY STAND IN FRONT OF CAMERAS AND RECITE WORDS WRITTEN BY OTHER PEOPLE--AND WE **WORSHIP** THEM FOR IT!

WE WATCH INTERVIEW PROGRAMS AND TRY TO FIGURE OUT WHO THEY REALLY **ARE**-- BECAUSE **WHOEVER** THEY ARE, WE WANT TO BE **JUST LIKE THEM**!

...SO, LIKE, I THINK PEOPLE SHOULD FOCUS THEIR POSITIVE ENERGY!
WHY--I FEEL THAT WAY ALSO!

SOME CITIZENS ARE ACTUALLY LUCKY ENOUGH TO MEET A MOVIE STAR IN **PERSON**--AN EXPERIENCE WHICH LEAVES THEIR LIVES **FOREVER ENRICHED**!

OUT OF MY WAY YOU WORTHLESS LITTLE PEON!
WOW! I CAN'T BELIEVE IT! SHE--SHE SPOKE TO ME!
TOM TOMORROW©'9

THIS MODERN WORLD by TOM TOMORROW

DEREGULATION WORKED SO WELL FOR THE SAVINGS AND LOAN INDUSTRY--
L.A. CO. DISTRICT ATTY.
NAME CHARLES KEATING JR
DOB 2-4-23
0665

--AND THE AIRLINES--
UNITED

--THAT THE BUSH ADMINISTRATION, AT THE URGING OF DAN QUAYLE'S COMPETITIVENESS COUNCIL, HAS NOW DECIDED TO EASE REGULATION ON AN EMERGING NEW INDUSTRY--
I JUST DON'T SEE WHY WE NEED TO MAKE SUCH A BIG FUSS...

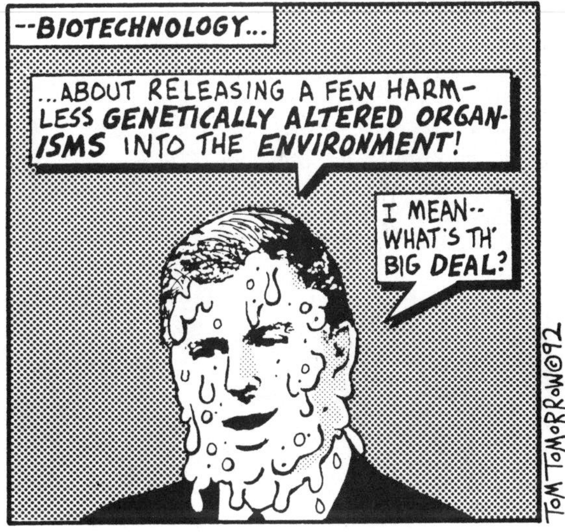
--BIOTECHNOLOGY...
...ABOUT RELEASING A FEW HARMLESS GENETICALLY ALTERED ORGANISMS INTO THE ENVIRONMENT!
I MEAN-- WHAT'S TH' BIG DEAL?
TOM TOMORROW©92

THIS MODERN WORLD by TOM TOMORROW

BILLY--DID YOU CLEAN YOUR **ROOM**?
UH HUH...
EXCUSE ME, YOUNG MAN...
DIET PEPSI
uh huh

I'M AN ATTORNEY FOR THE **PEPSI CORPORATION**...AND AS YOU CAN SEE FROM THIS CAN OF **DIET PEPSI**, THE PHRASE "UH HUH" IS NOW THE **TRADEMARKED PROPERTY** OF **PEPSICO, INC**!
DIET PEPSI
uh huh!

WE SPENT A **LOT OF MONEY** FORMULATING THIS CATCHY, MEMORABLE SLOGAN, BILLY--AND WE INTEND TO **PROTECT** OUR INVESTMENT! SO UNLESS YOU WANT YOUR FAMILY TO LOSE EVERYTHING THEY OWN IN A LENGTHY AND EXPENSIVE **TRADEMARK INFRINGEMENT SUIT**--
DIET PEPSI
uh huh!

--I'D SUGGEST YOU USE ALTERNATIVE AFFIRMATIVE PHRASES, SUCH AS 'YES', 'YOU BET', OR 'SURE THING'...OKAY, BILLY?
UH HUH--**ULP**! I MEAN--AH--**YOU BET**!
HEH, HEH! THAT'S A GOOD BOY!
DIET PEPSI
TOM TOMORROW©92

THIS MODERN WORLD by TOM TOMORROW

T.M.W.'s BOARD OF DIRECTORS HAS HIRED AN ***OUTSIDE MARKETING CONSULTANT***...

...WHAT THIS STRIP NEEDS TO DO IS TAP INTO THE VAST ***OFFICE HUMOR MARKET!*** WE NEED A ***GENTLY CYNICAL CATCHPHRASE***, SUITABLE FOR ***COFFEE MUGS*** AND ***DESK CALENDARS...***

...A MASS-PRODUCED MEANS FOR WORKERS IN STERILE CORPORATE ENVIRONMENTS TO EXPRESS A SMIDGEN OF INDIVIDUALITY... WITHOUT GETTING TOO FAR OUT OF LINE, OF COURSE...
HMM...I THINK I UNDERSTAND...
HOW'S THIS--

I HATE THIS JOB AND I WISH THE BOSS WOULD DIE!

HEH...THEY SAID YOU WERE A LITTLE CANTANKEROUS SOMETIMES...
NOT QUITE MARKETABLE ENOUGH FOR YOU? HOW ABOUT: "I WISH THE BOSS WOULD DIE PAINFULLY"?

TOM TOMORROW©92

THIS MODERN WORLD by TOM TOMORROW

IT'S THE YEAR 2029...
MOMMY--CAN WE GO OUT AND PLAY?
WELL, OF COURSE...

YOU KIDS DON'T HAVE TO STAY COOPED UP INSIDE ALL DAY LONG JUST BECAUSE THERE'S NO LONGER AN OZONE LAYER...

WE'VE JUST GOT TO REMEMBER THE SIMPLE PRECAUTIONS ONCE SUGGESTED BY A VERY WISE MAN...
FACTOR 300

...BIG HATS, DARK GLASSES, AND LOTS OF SUNSCREEN!
YOU TWO HAVE FUN!
TOM TOMORROW©92

THIS MODERN WORLD

by TOM TOMORROW

TRUE FACTS DEPT: DAN QUAYLE REJECTED AN HONORARY MEMBERSHIP IN THE ***GILLIGAN'S ISLAND FAN CLUB***, CITING "***ETHICAL CONSTRAINTS***..."

NO. ABSOLUTELY NOT.

WHILE WE'RE CERTAINLY RELIEVED THAT MR. QUAYLE ISN'T FOR SALE TO ANY SPECIAL INTEREST GROUP WITH A SO-CALLED "GIFT"...

...WE CAN'T HELP BUT WONDER WHAT MIGHT HAVE HAPPENED HAD THE V.P. BEEN A MAN OF ***LESSER INTEGRITY***...

COME ON, DAN! YOU GET A LAMINATED MEMBERSHIP CARD!
GILLIGAN'S ISLAND FAN CLUB
WHY DIDN'T YOU ***SAY*** SO?

...PERHAPS THE ***SKIPPER*** WOULD HAVE RECEIVED A HIGHLY SUSPICIOUS PROMOTION TO ***ADMIRAL***...

...THE ***PROFESSOR*** AND THE ***MOVIE STAR*** MIGHT HAVE "COINCIDENTALLY" BEEN NOMINATED TO HEAD THE DEPARTMENT OF ***EDUCATION*** AND THE ***N.E.A.***, RESPECTIVELY...

WE'D LIKE TO ***THANK*** YOU--
--FOR THESE ***UNEXPECTED HONORS***...

...AND PERHAPS ***GILLIGAN*** WOULD HAVE BEEN SELECTED AS THE ***RUNNING MATE*** FOR QUAYLE'S OWN EVENTUAL PRESIDENTIAL BID...

HEY--YOU GUYS THINK ***I'M*** A NIT-WIT? CHECK OUT ***THIS*** GUY!
LOOK OUT FOR THOSE ***COCONUTS***, MISTER BROKAW!

THIS MODERN WORLD

by TOM TOMORROW

IT BEGAN WITH HARRIS WOFFORD'S UNEXPECTED VICTORY IN PENNSYLVANIA... WHICH SENT REPUBLICAN STRATEGISTS ***SCURRYING***...

GOSH--PEOPLE ARE ***REALLY WORRIED*** ABOUT PAYING FOR THEIR HEALTH CARE!
I DON'T GET IT! WHY DON'T THEY JUST WITHDRAW MORE MONEY FROM THEIR ***TRUST FUNDS***?

DEMOCRATIC PRESIDENTIAL CANDIDATES QUICKLY EMBRACED THE HEALTH CARE ISSUE WITH THE ***MORAL FERVOR*** OF ONE WHOSE PARTY HAS BEEN OUT OF POWER FOR TWELVE YEARS...

HEALTH CARE!
HEALTH CARE!
HEALTH CARE!
HEALTH CARE!
HEALTH CARE!

FORCED TO FINALLY ADDRESS THE ISSUE, PRESIDENT BUSH EXPLAINED WHY A SYSTEM OF NATIONALIZED MEDICINE WOULD BE A ***BAD IDEA***--

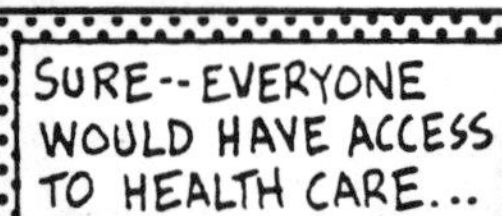
SURE--EVERYONE WOULD HAVE ACCESS TO HEALTH CARE...

...BUT THERE WOULD BE ***LONG LINES***!

--AND THEN UNVEILED HIS OWN ***BOLD, VISIONARY SOLUTION*** TO THE PROBLEM.

DON'T GET SICK.
TOM TOMORROW©92

THIS MODERN WORLD by TOM TOMORROW

FOR WEEKS, MEETINGS HAVE BEEN HELD IN SMOKE-FILLED BACK ROOMS...

HE'S THE PERFECT OUTSIDER CANDIDATE, GENTLEMEN!

POLLS HAVE BEEN TAKEN... FOCUS GROUPS CONDUCTED...

WOULD YOU CONSIDER VOTING FOR A SHORT, DICHROMATIC THIRD PARTY CANDIDATE WITH A BEAK?
SURE--AS LONG AS HE MADE A BLATANT APPEAL TO MY SELF-INTEREST!

FINALLY, AN EAGERLY-ANTICIPATED PRESS CONFERENCE IS HELD...

LADIES AND GENTLEMEN, I GIVE YOU THE NEXT PRESIDENT OF THE UNITED STATES--

--SPARKY™ THE WONDER PENGUIN!
...BECAUSE EVERYONE ELSE IS A WANKER!
SPARKY™
TOM TOMORROW©92

JOIN THE MOVEMENT, CITIZENS! VOTE MODERN! VOTE FOR SPARKY™!

THIS MODERN WORLD by TOM TOMORROW

SAY, BIFF--LET'S TALK ABOUT OUR RELATIONSHIP, USING POP PSYCHOLOGY BUZZ-WORDS!
THAT'S A GOOD IDEA, WANDA! AFTER ALL--THERE ARE ISSUES WHICH NEED TO BE ADDRESSED!

WE'VE GOT TO RESOLVE OUR INTERNALIZED CONFLICTS WITH A MINIMUM OF NEGATIVE INTERPERSONAL FEEDBACK!
YES, THAT'S TRUE--AND WE MUST BE SURE TO AVOID THE CLASSIC REACTIVE/RESPONSIVE MANIPULATION SCENARIOS!

PERHAPS THEN WE'LL BE ABLE TO SUCCESSFULLY NEGOTIATE A NEW PHASE IN EMOTIONAL STRUCTURING!
YES--WHILE ALLOWING SPACE FOR PERSONAL GROWTH OUTSIDE THE LINEAR STRUCTURES OF OUR CO-DEPENDENCY!

OH, BIFF--I FEEL SO MUCH BETTER WHEN WE INTERACT SO EFFECTIVELY!
ME TOO, WANDA!
I ONLY WISH I KNEW WHAT WE WERE TALKING ABOUT!
TOM TOMORROW©92

THIS MODERN WORLD by TOM TOMORROW

GOSH, WANDA--WITH THE COLLAPSE OF THE SOVIET UNION, THE CIA NEEDS A ***NEW MISSION!***

OH, BIFF--WILL YOU STOP PARROTING THE NEW YORK TIMES AND THINK FOR ***YOURSELF*** FOR A CHANGE?

VOTE FOR

SPARKY™

The New York Times

THE CIA WILL, IN ALL LIKELIHOOD, CONTINUE TO DO WHAT THEY HAVE ***ALWAYS*** DONE... MANIPULATING EVENTS IN THIRD WORLD COUNTRIES THROUGH WHATEVER ILLEGAL AND IMMORAL MEANS NECESSARY--
VOTE FOR
SPARKY

--TO ENSURE THAT GOVERNMENTS FRIENDLY TO U.S. ECONOMIC INTERESTS REMAIN IN POWER, WHILE LESS ***COOPERATIVE*** GOVERNMENTS DO ***NOT***... NO MATTER HOW BRUTAL A ***DICTATORSHIP*** THE FORMER MAY BE, NOR HOW ENLIGHTENED A ***DEMOCRACY*** THE LATTER...

VOTE FOR

ARKY™

THE END OF THE COLD WAR DOESN'T MEAN THE CIA NEEDS A NEW ***PURPOSE***, BIFF-- IT MEANS THEY NEED A NEW ***COVER STORY!***
VOTE FOR
SPARKY™
THAT ***PENGUIN***'S BEEN PUTTING IDEAS INTO YOUR HEAD AGAIN, HASN'T HE?
TOM TOMORROW©92

THIS MODERN WORLD by TOM TOMORROW

CAPTAIN'S LOG--STARDATE 1992. THE U.S.S. FREE ENTERPRISE HAS STALLED--LEAVING US ADRIFT...
MR. GREENSPAN--THOSE ENGINE THINGS--NEED 'EM WORKING!
I'VE TRIED TO STIMULATE 'EM, CAP'N--BUT THEY ARE NA' RESPONDIN'!

CAPTAIN--MESSAGE FROM STARFLEET--THEY SAY IF YOU CAN'T GET THE SHIP MOVING, THEY'LL REPLACE YOU WITH CAPTAIN CLIN-TON OR CAPTAIN TSONGAS!
TELL THEM--UNDERSTAND THEIR CONCERN--MADE SOME MISTAKES--BUT IT'S ALL UNDER CONTROL NOW--

SIR--RED ALERT! HOSTILE VESSEL MOVING IN-TO SENSOR RANGE!
THEY'RE HAILING US, SIR!
GREETINGS, CAPTAIN BUSH--

--FROM THE FAR RIGHT WING OF THE GALAXY! ARE YOU PREPARED TO SURRENDER?
SIR--HE'S FIRING HIS INVECTIVE WEAPONS! SHOULD WE RAISE OUR SHIELDS? RETURN FIRE?
NO--WE'LL IGNORE HIM--MAY-BE HE'LL JUST...GO AWAY...
WILL THE CAPTAIN'S BOLD PLAN SUCCEED? STAY TUNED!
TOM TOMORROW©92

THIS MODERN WORLD by TOM TOMORROW

SPARKY™ CONTINUES HIS QUEST FOR THE ***PRES-IDENCY***...

GEORGE BUSH TOLD YOU TO READ HIS ***LIPS***.

I DON'T ***HAVE*** ANY LIPS!

HIS INSURGENT CAMPAIGN RECEIVES LITTLE MEDIA ATTENTION--THE ***NEW YORK TIMES***, FOR INSTANCE, REFUSES TO EVEN ACKNOWLEDGE SPARKY™'S ***EXISTENCE***...

n and Brown Make Last Appeals

WANKERS

PHOTO ACCOMPANYING ***NEW YORK TIMES*** ELECTION STORY--

--AND THE ORIGINAL, UNCROPPED PHOTO.

THE MEDIA COVERAGE HE DOES RECEIVE TENDS TO BE DERISIVE AT BEST...
MY DOMESTIC POLICY IS SIMPLE--TAX THE RICH AND FEED THE HUNGRY.
I SEE--SO YOU'RE MAKING A PITCH FOR THE WACKO RADICAL FRINGE VOTE, EH? WELL--heh, heh--GOOD LUCK...
COMING UP NEXT: A REAL CANDIDATE DISCUSSES HIS PROPOSED CAPITAL GAINS TAX CUT.

MOST RECENTLY, SPARKY™ WAS THE TARGET OF A SUPERMARKET TABLOID'S SENSATIONAL-ISTIC ALLEGATIONS... BUT THROUGH IT ALL, HE PERSEVERES...
WHAT DO YOU SAY TO CHARGES THAT YOU'RE NOTHING MORE THAN A FICTIONAL CAR-TOON CHARACTER?
NEWS
SPARKY™ IS A "TOON"!
WELL--THAT MAY BE TRUE--BUT I DON'T BELIEVE IT DISQUALIFIES ME WHEN OUR LAST TWO PRESIDENTS HAVE BEEN COMPLETE JOKES!
© TOM TOMORROW

THIS MODERN WORLD by TOM TOMORROW

HEY, CITIZENS--CONFUSED ABOUT THE ***ISSUES***? MAYBE YOU SHOULD SPEND MORE TIME WATCHING THE ENDLESS PARADE OF ***COMMENTATORS*** AND ***EXPERTS*** ON THE ***TV NEWS***!

BLAH!
BLAH!
BLAH! BLAH!

THEY HAVE ***THREE PIECE SUITS*** AND ***IMPRESSIVE-SOUNDING CREDENTIALS***!

--JOINING US NOW FROM THE RESEARCH INSTITUTE FOR CULTURAL ANALYSIS OF POLICY STUDIES--

THEY REPRESENT THE ***WIDE SPECTRUM*** OF MAINSTREAM POLITICAL DISCOURSE--
--FROM THE ***MIDDLE OF THE ROAD***--
--TO THE ***EXTREME RIGHT WING***!

WE DON'T KNOW ABOUT ***YOU***, BUT ***WE'RE*** SURE GRATEFUL THAT THESE DISPASSIONATE ANALYSTS ARE WILLING TO SHARE THEIR KEEN, UNBIASED INSIGHTS WITH ***US***!

--STATISTICS ***CLEARLY*** PROVE THAT THE NIXON ADMINISTRATION'S FOREIGN POLICY WAS THE ***FINEST*** THIS COUNTRY HAS EVER SEEN!
TOM TOMORROW©91

THIS MODERN WORLD by TOM TOMORROW

AFTER A LONG DAY AT THE **STUDIO**, SPARKY™ IS GIVING T.M.W.'S MARKETING DIRECTOR A RIDE **HOME**...

...SO IT LOOKS LIKE THE REPUBLICANS HAVE MANAGED TO KILL OFF INTEREST IN THE 'OCTOBER SURPRISE' FOR NOW...

...WITH A LOT OF HELP FROM A COMPLIANT-- IF NOT **COMPLICIT**-- NEWS MEDIA...

...SUCH AS **NEWSWEEK** AND **THE NEW REPUBLIC**, BOTH OF WHOM PUBLISHED ERROR-RIDDEN AND MISLEADING COVER STORIES DENOUNCING GARY SICK'S BOOK ON THE SUBJECT--

--THOUGH NO ONE AT EITHER MAGAZINE HAD, AT THAT POINT, **READ** THE BOOK...

...AND OF COURSE WHEN SENATE REPUBLICANS RECENTLY MANAGED TO SCUTTLE AN INVESTIGATION WITH THE THREAT OF A FILIBUSTER THE NATIONAL NEWS MEDIA ALMOST ENTIRELY IGNORED THE STORY! WHAT A BUNCH OF WANKERS! I CAN'T BELIEVE--
AHEM! SAY, SPARKY™--

...WHEN YOU APPLIED FOR THE JOB OF A "CUTE, LOVABLE, EASILY MERCHANDISABLE CARTOON CHARACTER"--
--I WAS LYING THROUGH MY TEETH. I NEEDED THE WORK.
REALTOR
SPARKY™
TOM TOMORROW © '91

About the Author

Tom Tomorrow occasionally travels under the name "Dan Perkins," an obvious pseudonym. He lives in San Francisco with his significant POSSLQ, his Toshiba copier, and cats so plentiful a stick could not be shaken at them.